PIANO/VOCAL/CHORDS

The Collection of ROCK & ROLL MUSIC

Project Manager: Zobeida Pérez
Cover Illustration: Shigemi Shimada
Art Layout: Joe Klucar

CONTENTS

BLUEBERRY HILL

Words and Music by
AL LEWIS, VINCENT ROSE
and LARRY STOCK

A♭
E♭
still on Blue-ber-ry Hill
B♭7
and lin-gered un-til my dreams came
E♭
D♭7
E♭
A♭6
E♭
E♭6
true. The wind in the wil-low played
E♭maj7
A♭6
E♭
E♭6
E♭7
D7
love's sweet mel-o-dy; but all of those

Gm
D7
Gm
D7
G
vows we made were nev - er to be
Bb7
Eb7
Ab
Tho' we're a - part, you're part of me
Eb
Bb7
still for you were my thrill on Blue - ber - ry
1
Eb
Db7
Eb
Eb7
2
Eb
Ab6
Ebmaj7
Hill. I found my Hill.

DA DOO RON RON

Words and Music by
ELLIE GREENWICH, JEFF BARRY and PHIL SPECTOR

*Sing every time.

1.2.4.
To next strain
3.
A♭
B♭
E♭
E♭
name was Bill. *Da doo ron ron ron, da doo ron ron.
. . . end solo)
Bridge:
A♭
E♭
B♭
Yes, my heart stood still. Yes, his name was Bill.
E♭
A♭
B♭
E♭
And when he walked me home, da doo ron ron ron, da doo ron ron.
1.2.
D.S. 𝄋
3.
2. He
(bkgrd. vocals) Da

Verse 2:
He knew what he was doin' when he caught my eye.
Da doo ron ron ron, da doo ron ron.
He looked so quiet, but my, oh my.
Da doo ron ron ron, da doo ron ron.

Bridge 2:
Yes, he caught my eye.
Yes, but my, oh my.
And when he walked me home,
Da doo ron ron ron, da doo ron ron.

Verse 3:
(Instrumental solo)

Verse 4:
Picked me up at seven and he looked so fine.
Da doo ron ron ron, da doo ron ron.
Someday soon, I'm gonna make him mine.
Da doo ron ron ron, da doo ron ron.

Bridge 3:
Yes, he looked so fine.
Yes, I'll make him mine.
And when he walked me home,
Da doo ron ron ron, da doo ron ron.

BABY, IT'S YOU

Words and Music by
BURT BACHARACH, MACK DAVID
and BARNEY WILLIAMS

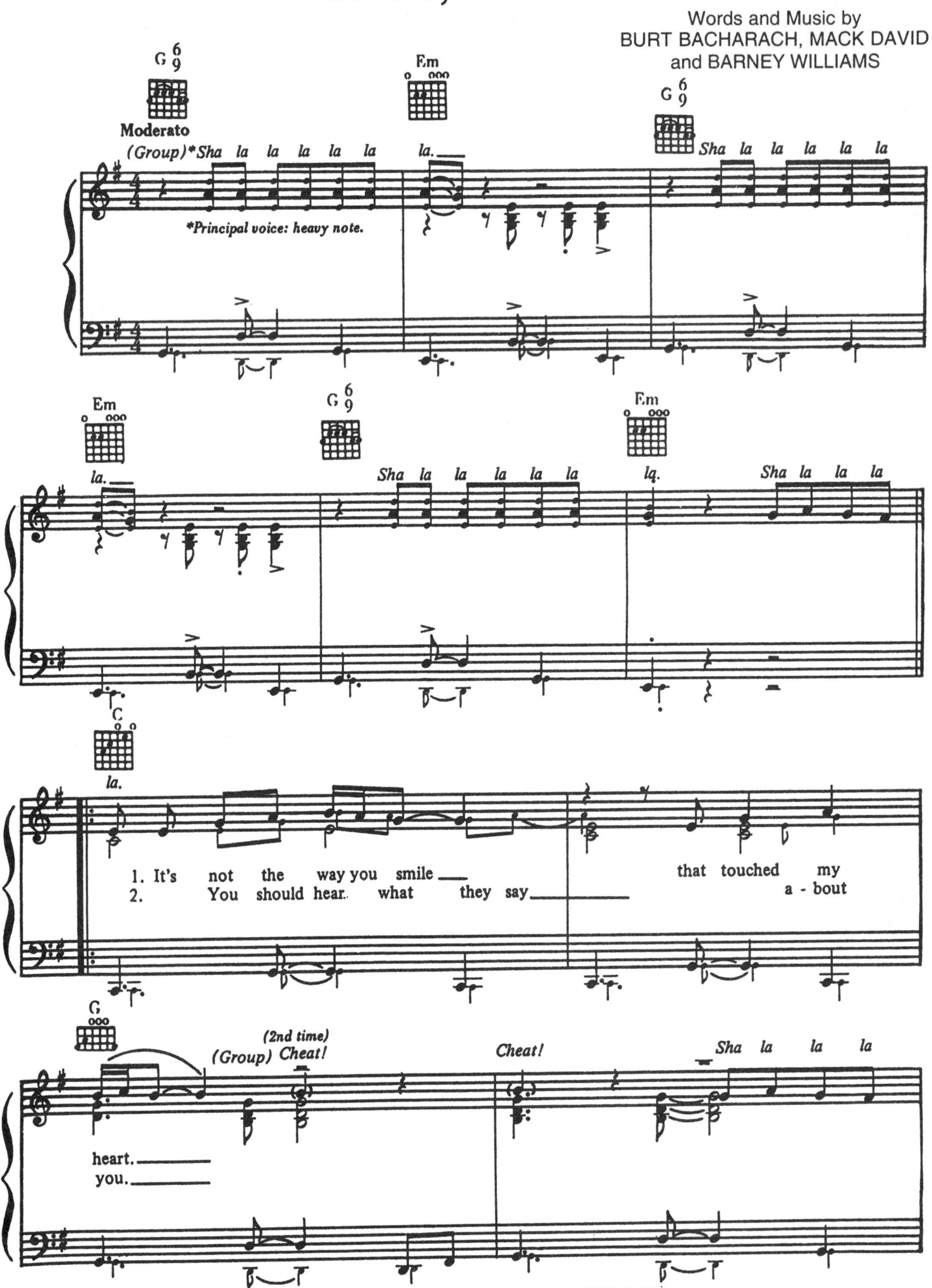

C
la.
It's not the way you kiss that tears me a -
They say, they say you've nev-er, nev-er, nev-er, ev - er been
G
(2nd time)
Cheat!
Cheat!
part.
true.
Oh, oh,
Oh, oh,
Em
1. man - y, man - y man-y nights go by,
2. & 3. does -n't mat - ter what they say,
Am
I sit a - lone at home and I cry o - ver
I know I'm gon - na love you an - y old way, what can I

G
Em
you; what can I do?
do, when it's true?
C
D7
5fr
Ah
Can't help my - self,
Don't want no - bod-y no - bod- y,
N.C.
'cause ba - by, it's
G 6 9
Em
Sha la la la la la la.
3rd time to Coda
G 6 9
Sha la la la la la
you.
Ba - by, it's
you.
1. Em
la. Sha la la la
2. Em
la.
C
3
Solo guitar 15va lower

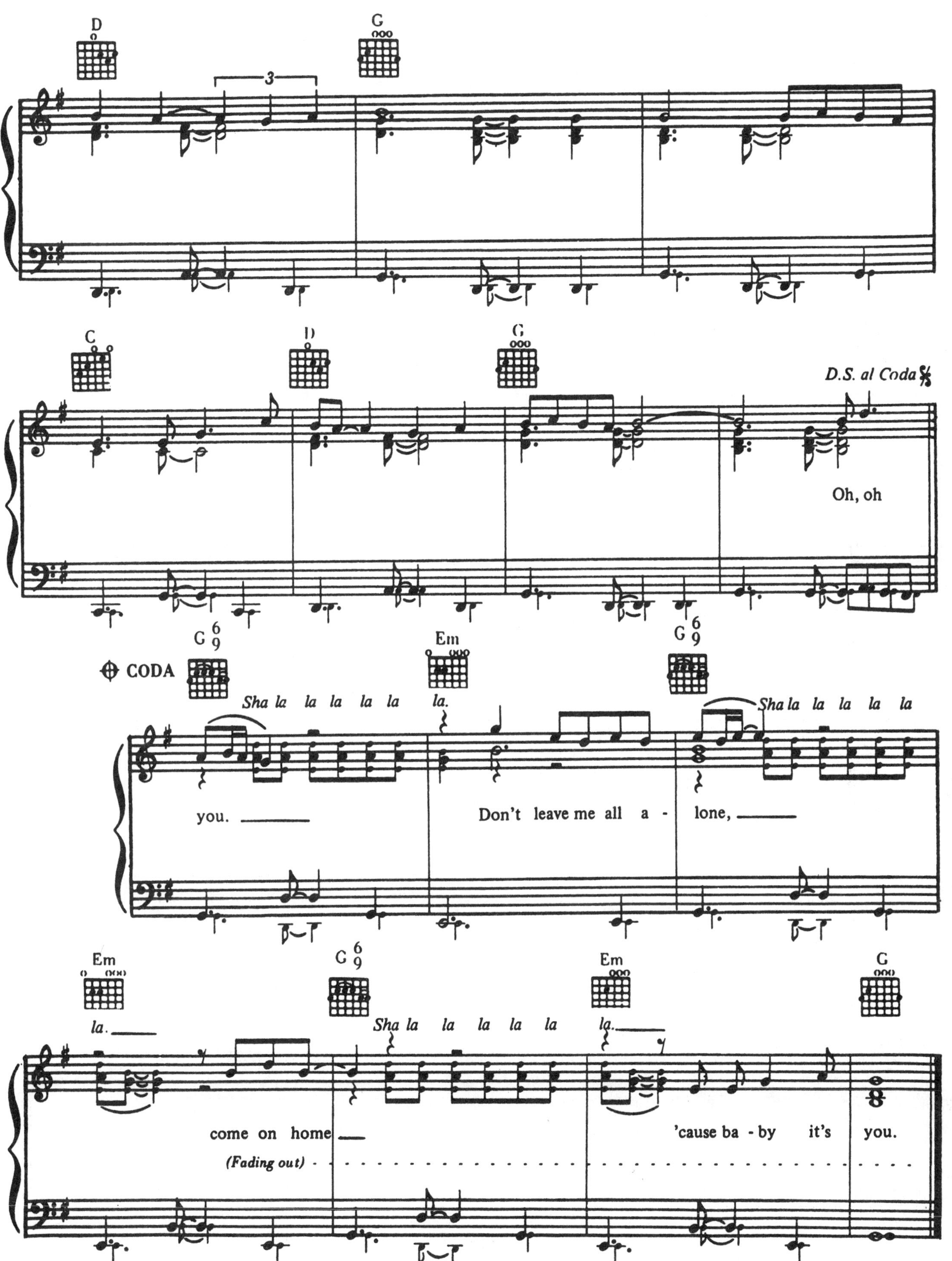
D
G
3
C
D
G
D.S. al Coda
Oh, oh
CODA
G 6/9
Em
Sha la la la la la la.
you.
Don't leave me all a - lone,
Sha la la la la la
la.
come on home
(Fading out)
Sha la la la la la la.
'cause ba - by it's you.

BE-BOP BABY

Words and Music by
PEARL LENDHURST

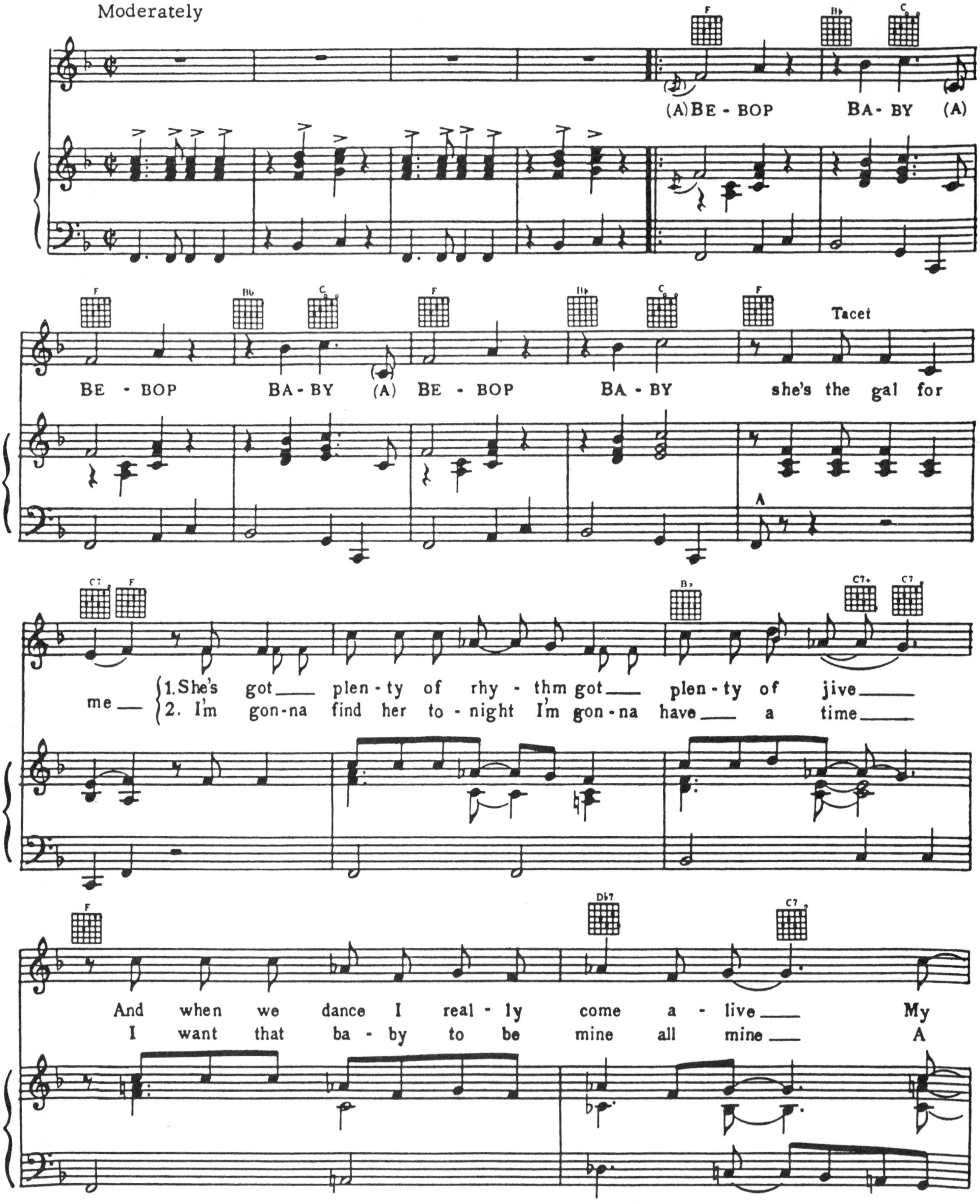

Moderately

F B♭ C
(A) BE - BOP BA - BY (A)

F B♭ C F B♭ C F Tacet
BE - BOP BA - BY (A) BE - BOP BA - BY she's the gal for

C7 F B♭ C7+ C7
me — 1. She's got — plen - ty of rhy - thm got — plen - ty of jive —
2. I'm gon - na find her to - night I'm gon - na have — a time —

F D♭7 C7
And when we dance I real - ly come a - live — My
I want that ba - by to be mine all mine — A

F F7

— love for her is so — ten - der and sweet, — My
big day is com in' for my ba - by and me, — The

B♭ B♭m7 F

heart starts pound - ing ev - 'ry time we meet —
day she says — she be - longs to me —
My BE - BOP BA - BY

F7 B♭ B♭m

still in her teens Just as sweet as she can be — My

F D7 G7-9 C7

BE - BOP BA - BY in her old blue jeans is the BE - BOP BA - BY for me

F D7 G7 C7 F F

— A BE - BOP BA - BY for me. — —

1. 2.

BE MY BABY

Words and Music by
ELLIE GREENWICH, JEFF BARRY and PHIL SPECTOR

G♯7
C♯7
So won't you say you love me? I'll make you so proud of me.
Oh, since the day I saw you, I have been wait - ing for you.
F♯7
B
We'll make 'em turn their heads ev - 'ry place we go.
You know I will a - dore you till e - ter - ni - ty.
So won't you please
Chorus:
E
C♯m
be my lit - tle ba - by?
(Be my, be my ba - by,) (my one and
A
Say you'll be my dar - lin'.
Be my ba - by
on - ly ba - by.) (Be my, be my ba - by,)

1.
2.
B7
now,
(my one and
woh, oh, oh, oh.
on - ly ba - by.)
woh, oh, oh, oh,
on - ly ba - by.)
E
F♯m7
B
oh.
E
F♯m7
B
So come on and
E
C♯m
please
(Be my, be my ba - by,)
Be my lit-tle ba - by.
(my one and

A
Say you'll be my dar - lin'.
on - ly ba - by.)
(Be my, be my ba - by,)
Be my ba - by
B7
now,
(my one and on - ly ba - by.)
woh, oh, oh, oh.
N.C.
Perc.:
E
(oh.)
(Be my, be my ba - by,)
Be my lit-tle ba - by,
C#m
(my one and on - ly ba - by.)
oh,
A
(Be my, be my ba - by,)
oh,
B7
(my one and on - ly ba - by.)
woh, oh, oh, oh.
Repeat ad lib. and fade

BABY
(You've Got What It Takes)

Words and Music by
CLYDE OTIS and MURRAY STEIN

Eb
You know it takes a lot of kiss-in' To make a ro-mance sweet,
(Opt.)
(simile)
Ab7
Eb
Ooh, It takes a lot of lov-in' To make my life com-plete;
(Opt.)
Bb7
Ab7
Bb7
And it takes a lot of wo-man To knock me off my feet,
Ab7
Bb7
Eb
And BA-BY, You've Got What It Takes.
Ab7
Eb
I say Mm

Ab7
Bb7
Uh-huh-huh, Mm
You know you've got just what it takes. Be-cause it
Eb
takes more than an ef-fort
To stay a-way from you,
It takes
(Opt.)
Ab7
Eb
more than a life-time
To prove that I'll be true;
But it
Bb7
Ab7
Bb7
Ab7
takes some-bod-y spe-cial
To make me say, "I do,"
And BA-BY,
Bb7
1 Eb
Bb7
2 Eb
You've Got What It Takes.
Well, now, it

BEYOND THE SEA

(La Mer)

English Words by
JACK LAWRENCE

Music and French Words by
CHARLES TRENET

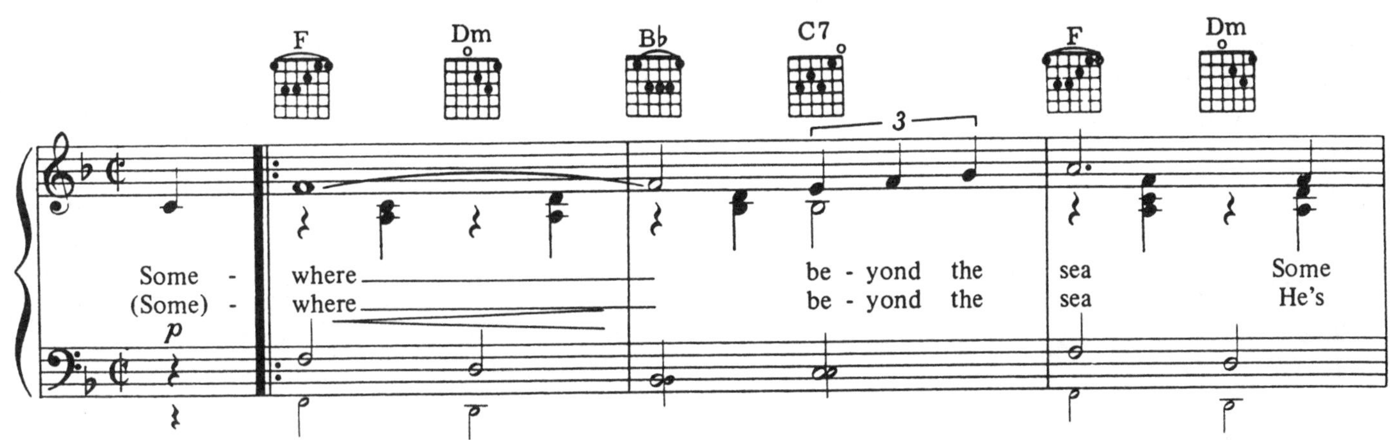

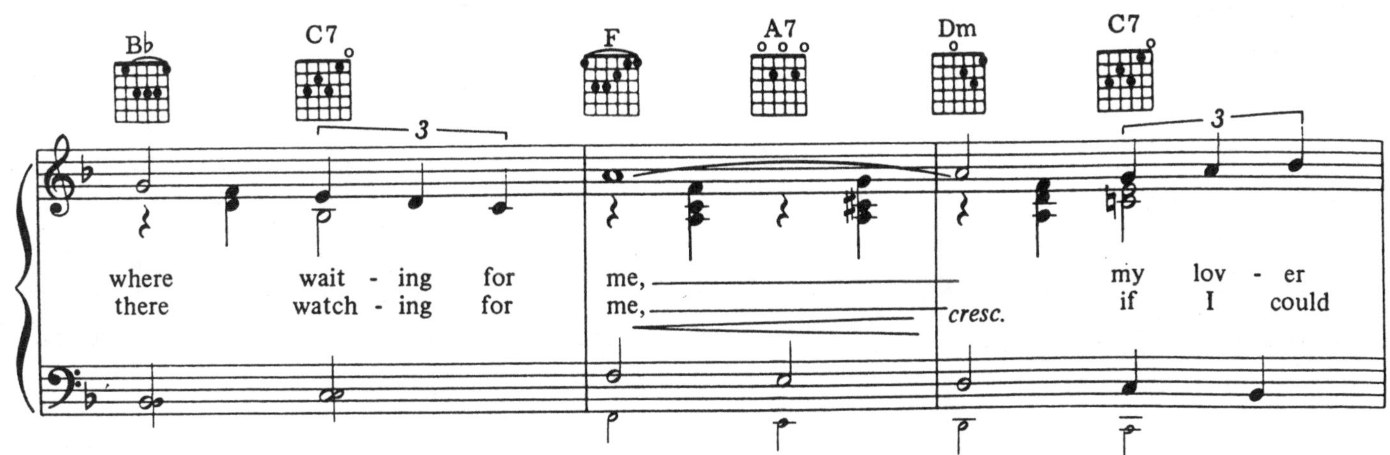

F
Dm
B♭
D7
Gm
3fr
C7
Gdim
5fr
Dm
B♭
3
stands on gold - en sands
fly like birds on high
And watch - es the ships that go
Then straight to his arms I'd go
1.
G7
C
C7
2.
Gm7
3fr
C7
F
E7
sail - ing; Some -
sail - ing. It's
A
F♯m
2fr
D6
E7
A
F♯m
2fr
D6
E7
3
3
far be - yond a star, it's near be - yond the
3
A
G7
C
Am
F
G7
3
moon, I know be - yond a
piu espr.
3

C
Am
Dm
G7
C
C7
Am
C7
doubt, my heart will lead me there soon. We'll
dim.
p
F
Dm
B♭
C7
F
Dm
B♭
C7
meet be - yond the shore, we'll kiss just as be -
F
A7
Dm
C7
F
Dm
B♭
D7
fore, Hap - py we'll be be - yond the sea
cresc.
Gm
3fr
C7
Gdim
5fr
Dm
B♭
G7
C7
F
and nev - er a - gain I'll go sail - ing.

THE BIRDS AND THE BEES

Words and Music by
HERB NEWMAN

Moderately, with a beat
G Em Am7 D7 G Em
mf
D7 G D7
Let me tell ya 'bout the birds and the bees and the flow - ers and the trees and the
G
moon up a-bove and a thing called love
D7
Let me tell ya 'bout the stars in the sky and a girl and a guy and the

G

way they could kiss, on a night _ like this. ___

G7 C

When I look in - to your big brown eyes ___

G

it's so ver - y plain to see ________

Em7 A7

that it's time you learned _ a - bout the

D7
Am7
D7
facts of life starting from "A" to "Z". Let me tell ya 'bout the
G
D7
birds and the bees and the flow-ers and the trees and the moon up a-bove
1 G
and a thing called love.
2 G
Am7
Gmaj7
Let me tell ya 'bout the love.

BOBBY SOX TO STOCKINGS

Words and Music by
RUSSELL FAITH,
CLARENCE WAY KEHNER
and RICHARD DiCICCO

F
Em
Dm7
G7
once shy lit - tle sleep - y head learns a - bout love and its
Cmaj7
C6
Am7
D7
Dm7
lilt, you can bet that the change is more than from cot - ton to silk.
G7
Cmaj7
C6
Dm7
G7
If a miss wants to be kissed in - stead of
Cmaj7
C6
Dm7
G7
Cmaj7
C6
cud - dled, and to this you are in

Dm7
G7
Dm7
G7
doubt as what to do.
When a
F
B7♭9
B7
Em
girl chang - es from bob - by sox to stock -
A7
Fdim
A7
Dm7
G7
ings, then she's old e - nough to give her heart a -
1
Cmaj7
C6
Dm7
G7
2
C
way.
When a
way.

BLUE VELVET

Words and Music by
BERNIE WAYNE and LEE MORRIS

Cm
F7
B♭
Dm
She wore blue vel - vet,
Cm7
F7(♭9)
B♭
Cm7
blu - er than vel - vet were her eyes,
warm - er than May her ten - der
F7
Fm7
sighs, love was ours.
B♭9
E♭
(appassionato)
E♭m7
Ours, a love I held tight - ly,
ff
(appassionato)

B♭
B♭7
feel - ing the rap - ture grow,
E♭
E♭m7
Dm7
D♭dim7
like a flame burn - ing bright - ly.
But when she left,
Cm7
F7
rit.
B♭
a tempo
Dm
gone was the glow of blue vel - vet.
Cm7
F7(♭9)
B♭
Cm7
But in my heart there'll al-ways be,
pre - cious and warm, a mem-o -

F7
Fm
ry through the years,
3
3
Bb9
Eb
F7(#5)
molto espressivo
and I still can see blue vel - vet through my
3
mp
subito molto espressivo
rit.
1.
2.
Bb6
G7(b9)
Cm
F7
Bb6
a tempo
tears.
She wore
tears.
a tempo
mf

BUILD ME UP BUTTERCUP

Words and Music by
TONY McCAULEY and
MICHAEL D'ABO

C
E7(#5)
of all (worst of all) you nev - er call ba - by when you
F
G11
say you will (say you will) but I love you still; I need you
C
G7
C7
(I need you) more than an - y - one dar - ling you
F
Fm
E7(#5)
Fm6
C
know that I have from the start. So build me up (build me up) but -

To Coda
G7
F
C
Dm7
C
G
- ter - cup don't break my heart.
I'll be
To
C
G
B♭
F
ov - er at ten, you tell me time and a - gain but you're late,
you I'm a toy but I could be the boy you a - dore.
C
Dm
Dm9
G7
C
G
I wait a - round and then: I run to the door, I can't take
If you just let me know: and though you're un - true I'm at - tract -
B♭
F
C
Dm
C
an - y more, it's not you, you let me down a - gain.
- ed to you all the more why do I need you so?

Dm
Dm
G7
C
Dm
Em
Ba - by ba - by
try to find
a lit - tle time and
A7
Dm
A7
Dm
D7
I'll make you hap - py, I'll be home, I'll be be - side the 'phone, wait - ing for
2nd time D.S. al Coda
G
Gsus
G13
G9sus
G13
G11
G9sus
G13
you.
Oo
Oo
Why do you
CODA
F
C
Dm7
C
Don't break my heart.
R.H.
L.H.

CALIFORNIA DREAMIN'

Words and Music by
JOHN PHILLIPS and
MICHELLE PHILLIPS

California Dreamin' - 3 - 1

E7
Am
G
To Coda
F
G
Bm7
Cal - i - for - nia dream-in'
On such a win-ter's day.
E7
Am
G
F
G
Bm7
Stopped in - to a church,
I passed a - long the way.
E7
F
C
E7
Am
F
E
Dm6
Oh, I got down on my knees,
And I pre-tend to pray.
E7
Am
G
F
G
Bm7
You know the preach-er likes the cold,
He knows I'm gon - na stay.

E7
Am
G
F
G
Cal - i - for - nia dream - in'
On such a win - ter's
Bm7
E7
D.S. al Coda
day.
All the leaves are
CODA
F
G
On such a win - ter's
Am
G
F
G
Am
G
F
G
day. (Cal - i - for - nia dream - in') On such a win - ter's day. (Cal - i - for - nia dream - in') On such a win - ter's
Fmaj7
Am
day.

DEDICATED TO THE ONE I LOVE

Words and Music by
LOWMAN PAULING and
RALPH BASS

D9
Em
Bm
Am7
cause it's hard for me my ba - by.
And the dark-est hour
D7
G
D7
is just be - fore dawn.
Each
While
D9
G
D7
night be - fore you go to bed
I'm far a - way from you
My ba - by
D7
G
Whis - per a lit - tle prayer for me my

D
D7
D9
To Coda I
ba - by.
(Yeah)
And then tell
Be cause it's
Gdim7
G
all the stars a - bove.
This is de - di -
no chord
To Coda II
G
ca - ted to the one I love.
Life can nev - er be ex -
act - ly like we want it to be, I could be sat - is -

fied knowing you love me. There's one thing I want you to
do especially for me And it's something that
Am
A7
D9
D7
D.S. al Coda I
ev-'ry-body needs.
CODA I
Em
Bm
Am7
hard for me my baby, And the dark-est hour

D7 G7 Bm Em

is just be-fore dawn. There's one thing I want you to

G Bm C Bm no chord E♭

do es-pe-cial-ly for me, and it's some-thing

D7

ev-'ry-bod-y needs.

D.S. al Coda II

CODA II

Em Em C

love This is de-di-ca-ted to the one I love This is de-di-

CANDY MAN

Words and Music by
NEIL FREDERICKS and
BEVERLY ROSS

Moderately fast swing
D7
D♭7
C7
f
G
Come on ba -
G6
- by,
let me take you by the hand.
C9
Come on
sug - ar,
let me take you by the hand.
G6
D7
You're for me,

C7
G
hon-ey let me be
all your own can - dy,
G7
G#7
can - dy,
your can - dy man.
A7
D
Well, hey there sweet
thing.
D7
I love your
hon-ey lov - in'
ways.
Hey there sweet
G7
thing,
I love your
hon-ey lov - in',

D
hon-ey lov-in' ways.
So come to me,
A7
G7
and I'll let you be
all my own
D
can - dy, can - dy,
my can - dy man.
A7
D
N.C.
G/D
Come on woman,
I'm gon-na treat you right.
D N.C.
G/D
D N.C.
D7
I'll give you can - dy kiss - es
ev-'ry sin - gle night,

G7
G
so come on, ba - by,
I love your
D
hon - ey lov - in', your hon - ey lov - in' ways.
A7
Yes, I do,
so come to me,
G7
D
yeah. I'll let you be
all my own can - dy, can -
N.C.
D
G/D D
dy,
my can - dy man.

CARA MIA

Italian Lyrics by GAGIS

Original Words and Music by
TULIO TRAPANI and LEE LANGE

Db
Bbm6
F
C7-9
Fmaj7
F6
All I want is you for ev - er - more, To
Bbm6
F
Db7
C7
C7-9
have, to hold, to love, a - dore.
F
Am
Bb
F
CA - RA MI - A mine say those words di - vine,
Bbm6
F
1 Gm7
C7
F
C7-9
I'll be your love till the end of time.
2 Gm7
Gb7
F
end of time.
cresc.
rit.

CARRIE-ANNE

Words and Music by
ALLAN CLARKE, TONY HICKS
and GRAHAM NASH

F/A G7 C Dm/A C F/A C
you played a mon - i - tor then you played with old - er boys and pre - fects.
nev - er car - ing, you lost your charm as you were ag - ing.
I'll be your teach - er, when the les - son's o - ver you'll be with me.
Fmaj7/A G7sus G7 C F G/F#
What's the at - trac - tion in what they're do - ing.
Where is your mag - ic dis - ap - pear - ing.
Then I'll hear the oth - er peo - ple say - ing.
Hey Car - rie - Anne
G C F G7
what's your game now, can an - y - bod - y play?
C F G C F
Hey Car - rie - Anne what's your game now, can an - y - bod - y
To Coda

1
2
G7
G7
F
play?
play?
You're so
so
Bb
F
like a wom-an to me
(So like a wom-an to me)
so
Bb
(so)
so
like a wom-an to me.
(Like a wom-an to me.)
G7sus
G7
G7sus
G7
C6
Hey Car-rie - Anne

G
C
F
G7
what's your game — now, can a - ny - bod - y play?
C
F
G/F♯
G
C
F
Hey Car - rie - Anne — what's your game — now, can an - y - bod - y
G7
D.S. al Coda
play?
CODA
G7
play?
F
C/E
G7
C
Car - rie - Anne Car - rie - Anne — Car - rie-Anne. Car - rie Anne.

CHAPEL OF LOVE

Words and Music by
JEFF BARRY, ELLIE GREENWICH
and PHIL SPECTOR

G
1. Spring is here, the sky is blue,
2. Bells will ring, the sun will shine,
Am
D
Birds all sing as if they knew. To -
I'll be his and he'll be mine. We'll
day's the day we'll say I do. And we'll nev - er be
love un - til the end of time And we'll nev - er be
D7
lone - ly an - y - more.
lone - ly an - y - more.
D. C. al Fine

DO WAH DIDDY DIDDY

Words and Music by
JEFF BARRY and ELLIE GREENWICH

D7
fine, (Yeah, yeah) He looked good, he looked fine, and I near-ly lost my mind. Be-
door, (Yeah, yeah) We walked on to my door, and he
mf
D7 G Em
stayed a lit-tle more. My, my, my, my, I knew we were fall-in' in
more broadly
C D7
love, My, my, my, my, I told him all the things I was
cresc.
G C G
dream-in' of. Now we're to-geth-er near-ly ev-'ry sin-gle day, Sing-in'
mf
f

C
G
DO WAH DID - DY DID - DY, down did - dy do;
We're so hap - py and that's
mf
C
G
how we're gon - na stay, Sing - in' DO WAH DID - DY DID - DY, down did - dy do. 'Cause I'm
f
his, (Yeah, yeah) and he's mine, (Yeah, yeah) Well, I'm his and he's mine and the
G
C
G
Repeat and Fade
wed - din' bells will chime, Sing - in' DO WAH DID - DY DID - DY, down did - dy do,

DOWNTOWN

Key of G (D-D)

Words and Music by
TONY HATCH

Medium rock
Piano
mf
* G
Gmaj.7
C
D7
G
1. When you're a - lone_ and life is mak - ing you lone - ly, you can al-ways go_
2. Don't hang a - round_ and let your prob-lems sur - round_ you, there are mov-ie shows_
3. (Instrumental to ☆.)
mp - mf
C
D
G
Gmaj.7
C
D7
DOWN-TOWN. When you've got wor - ries, all the noise and the hur - ry seems to
DOWN-TOWN. May - be you know_ some lit - tle plac - es to go_ to where they

*Chord names and diagrams for guitar.

G
C
D
G
help, I know._ DOWN-TOWN. Just list - en to the mu - sic of the
nev - er close._ DOWN-TOWN. Just list - en to the rhy - thm of a
☆ And you may find some - bod - y kind to
f
Em
G
Em
traf - fic in the ci - ty. Ling - er on the side-walk where the ne - on signs are pret - ty.
gen - tle Bos - sa No - va. You'll be danc - ing with 'em too be - fore the night is ov - er,
help and un - der - stand you. Some - one who is just like you and needs a gen - tle hand to
Bm
C
How can you lose?
hap - py a - gain.
guide them a - long.
1
2 The lights_ are much bright - er __ there,_ you can for -
(3) So, may - be I'll see you_ there,_ we can for -
mf
mp
Em7
A
Em7
A
G
Gmaj.7
get all your trou - bles, for - get all your cares._ So go DOWN - TOWN,
get all our trou - bles, for - get all our cares._ So go DOWN - TOWN,
f

Am7
D6
D9
G
Gmaj.
Am7
D6
D9
things-'ll be great_ when you're DOWN - TOWN. No fin - er place,_ for sure,
where all the lights_ are bright DOWN - TOWN, wait - ing for you ___ to - night
things-'ll be great_ when you're DOWN - TOWN. Don't wait a min - ute more
ff
G
Gmaj.7
Am7
D6
D9
1.2.G
Am7
DOWN - TOWN. Ev - 'ry - thing's wait - ing for you
DOWN - TOWN. You're gon - na be ___ al - right now
DOWN - TOWN. Ev - 'ry - thing's wait - ing for
fff
Gmaj.7
Am7
Gmaj.7
Am7
Gmaj.7
Am7
3. G
Am7
DOWN - TOWN.
you
mf
G
Am7
G
Am7
G
Am7
Repeat and fade
Gmaj.7
DOWN - TOWN._ DOWN - TOWN._

DON'T LET THE SUN CATCH YOU CRYING

Words and Music by
GERARD MARSDEN, FRED MARSDEN,
LES CHADWICK and LES MAGUIRE

E7
Am
E7
Em
bro - ken to - night
but to - mor-row in the morn - ing light,
Dm7
G7
Cmaj7
Fmaj7
don't let the sun catch you cry - ing.
Cmaj7
Fmaj7
Cmaj7
The night - time
It may be
Fmaj7
Cmaj7
Fmaj7
shad - ows dis - ap - pe - ar
hard to dis - cov - er
3

Cmaj7
Fmaj7
G
and with them go all your tears.
that you've been left for an - oth -
G7
Am
E7
For the morn-ing will bring joy for
er But don't for - get that life's a game and it
Am
E7
Em
Dm7
G7
ev - 'ry girl and boy. So,
al-ways comes a - gain. Oh,
don't let the sun catch you
Cmaj7
To Coda
Fmaj7
Cmaj7
cry - ing.

Fmaj7
F#m7♭5
G
Am
We know that cry-ing's not a bad thing.
Dm
G7
But stop your cry - ing when the birds sing.
D.S. al Coda
CODA
Fmaj7
Don't let the
Cmaj7
Fmaj7
Cmaj7
sun catch you cry - ing, oh no, oh oh oh.

ENCHANTED

Words and Music by
BUCK RAM

Eb
Fm
Bb7
all the world's a - glow. They ought to know.
Eb
Ab
When you touch a star then you real - ly are en -
Love is ec - sta - sy, it's di - vine to be en -
Eb
chant - ed. Find the seed and
chant - ed, when your dreams are
Bb7
plant it. Love will make it
slant - ed through a lov - er's

E♭
A♭
E♭
E♭7
A♭
grow
eyes.
It's real - ly grand when you stand hand in
E♭
hand with your lov - er and thrill to the won - ders of
F7
night. And days too will a - maze you and soon you dis - cov - er your
B♭7
E♭
dreams run to dreams in con - tin - u - ous flight. Love is ec - sta - sy,

A♭
E♭
it's di - vine to be en - chant - ed.
B♭7
When your dreams are slant - ed
E♭
through a lov - er's eyes.
B♭7
E♭

ENDLESSLY

Words and Music by
CLYDE OTIS and BROOK BENTON

Bb
Bdim7
that's how I will
F
Dm
F
love you, darling,
Bb
F
endlessly.
Bb
F
Softer than the gentle breezes

B♭
and strong - er than a wild oak
F
tree.
B♭
That's how
Bdim7
F
Dm
I will hold you,
F
B♭
F
dar - ling, end - less - ly.

Bb
F
Gm
3fr
C7
C7#5
F
Bb
Am
Dm
3
3
Oh, my love
you are my
heav - en,
you are my king - dom,
you are my crown.
Oh, my love
you're all I prayed for;

G7
you were made for these arms to sur -
3
C7
round.
F
Faith - ful as a
B♭
F
morn - ing sun - rise and
sa - cred as a love can be,

Bb
Bdim7
that's how I will
F
Dm
F
love you, darling,
Bb
1 F
endlessly.
2 F
F
Repeat and Fade
ly. Endlessly. Endless-

FERRY 'CROSS THE MERSEY

Words and Music by
GERARD MARSDEN

With a beat

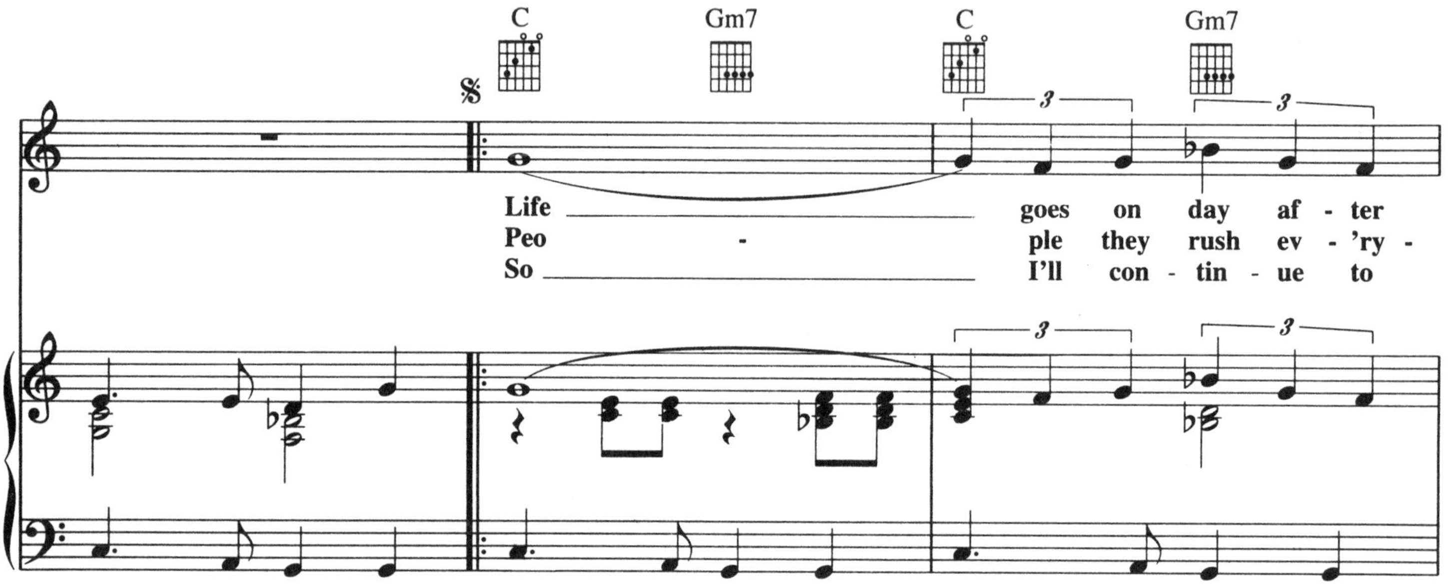
C
Gm7
C
Gm7
Life goes on day af - ter
Peo - ple they rush ev - 'ry -
So I'll con - tin - ue to

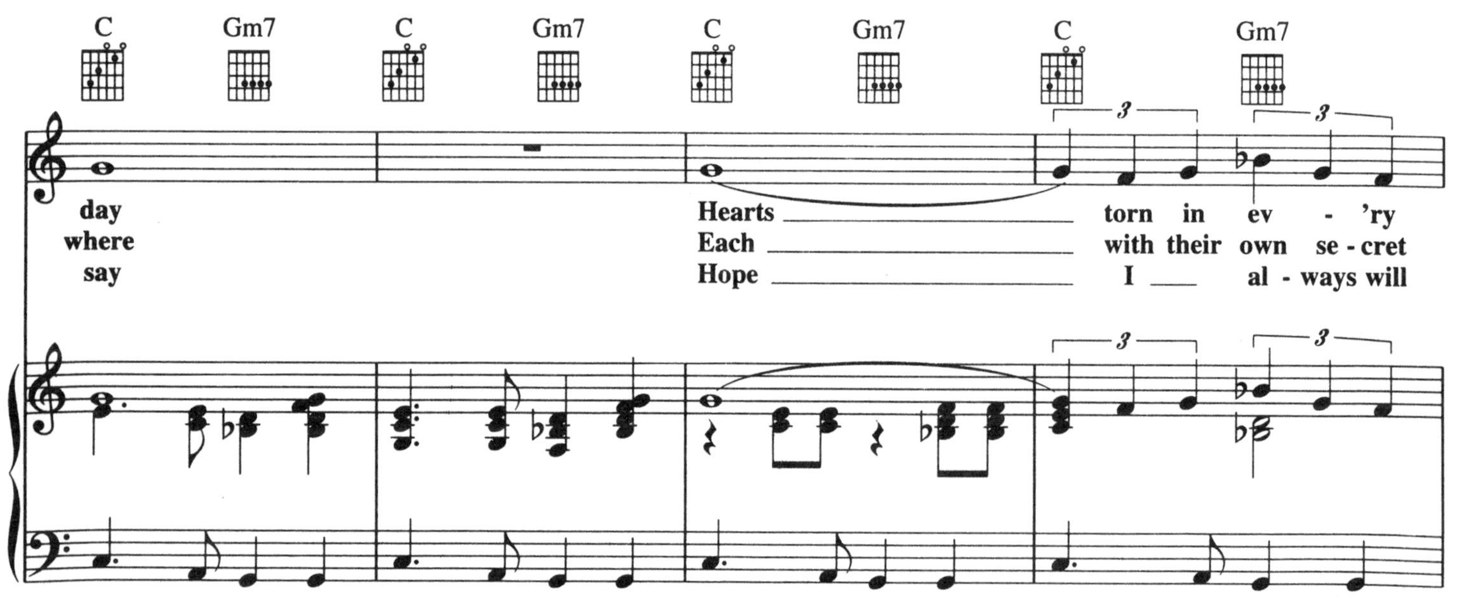
C
Gm7
C
Gm7
C
Gm7
C
Gm7
day
where
say
Hearts torn in ev - 'ry
Each with their own se - cret
Hope I al - ways will

C
Gm7
C
Gm7
G7
C
way
care
stay
So fer - ry cross the
So fer - ry cross the
So fer - ry cross the
Em
Dm
G7
To Coda
Mer - sey 'Cos this land's the place I love And here I'll
Mer - sey And al - ways take me there The place I
Mer - sey 'Cos this land's the place I love And here I'll
1
C
Gm7
C
Gm7
2
C
stay
love
3
3
Dm
G7
C
Peo - ple a - round ev - 'ry cor - ner

Dm
G7
C
Dm
G7
They seem to smile and say
We don't care what your
Em
D7
G7
D.S. al Coda
name is boy
We'll nev - er send you a - way
CODA
C
Gm7
C
Gm7
C
Gm7
stay
And here I'll
stay
C
Gm7
C
Gm7
C
Gm7
C
Here I'll
stay.

(Now And Then There's)

A FOOL SUCH AS I

Words and Music by
BILL TRADER

E7
F
C
F/A
Ab7b5
dream a lit - tle dream, as years go by. Now and
C/G
G#dim7
Am
Dm
Dm7b5
G7
C
then, there's a fool such as I.
C7
Gm7/C
C7
F
F#dim7
Now and then, there's a fool such as
C/G
F/A
Fm6/Ab
6fr
C
C#dim7
G/D
I am o - ver you. You taught me how to

D7 D♯dim7 Em C♯dim7 Dm A7 Fm6/A♭ G7 N.C.

love, and now you say that we are through. I'm a

C E7 F

fool, but I'll love you, dear, un - til the day I

C F/A A♭7♭5 C/G G♯dim7 Am Dm Dm7♭5 G7

die. Now and then, there's a fool such as

1 C Dm G7 N.C. 2 C F C

I. Par - don I.

GOIN' OUT OF MY HEAD

Words and Music by
TEDDY RANDAZZO and
BOBBY WEINSTEIN

2.
Cmaj7
Dm7/G
G7
Cmaj7
Dm7
-ist. Go - in' out of my head over you, out of my
Cmaj7
Dm7
C
F6
C
F6
C
F6
head over you, out of my head day and night, night and day and
C
F6
C
D
Fm6
night wrong or right. I must think of a way into your
C
Cdim
G
G7
F♯dim/G
heart. There's no rea-son why my be-ing shy should keep us a -
G
Cm7
Cmaj7
Repeat and fade
dim.
part. And I think I'm go-ing out of my head. Yes I

GONNA GET ALONG WITHOUT YA NOW

Words and Music by
MILTON KELLEM

Dm7
Gm7
3fr
C9
girl
boy
in town
And ya
nev - er cared if it
got me down.
You
lost my pride,
Did - n't have much mon - ey but I
real - ly tried.
It
Fmaj7
Dm7
Gm7
3fr
had me wor - ried, al - ways
on my guard,
But ya
laughed at me
'cause I
made you hap - py when you
made me cry,
And ya
broke my heart
so I
C9
To Coda
F
tried so hard!
said good - bye!
Boom, boom,
Boom,
Melody
Am
Gm7
3fr
C7
Fmaj7
boom,
Gon - na
get a - long with - out ya now.
Boom,
Melody

F
Am
Gm7
3fr
C7
boom, Boom, boom, Gon - na get a - long with - out ya now.
Fmaj7
Am
Dm7
(Play)
Gm7
3fr
C9
D.S. al Coda
F
Am7
Gm7
3fr
C7
Fmaj7
boom, Boom, boom, Gon-na get a - long with-out ya now. Boom,
Melody
Melody

GOOD GOLLY MISS MOLLY

Words and Music by
ROBERT BLACKWELL
and JOHN MARASCALCO

C+
F
B♭7
F
B♭7
Well, from the ear - ly, ear - ly morn-in' to the ear - ly ear - ly night, When I
F
caught Miss Mol - ly rock - in' at the House of Blue Lights, Ooh Good Gol - ly Miss
B♭7
F
Mol - ly, Yeah you sure like a ball. When you're rock - in' and - a -
C7
B♭7
F
C+
roll - in' Can't you hear your Mom - ma call? Well, now

F
B♭7
F
B♭7
Mom - ma, Pop - pa told me "Son, you'd bet - ter watch your step," What I
knew a - bout Miss Mol - ly, Got - ta watch my dad-dy my - self. Good Gol - ly Miss
Mol - ly Yeah you sure like a ball,
When you're shak - in' and a
C7
shout - in' Can't you hear your Mom-ma call?
E♭

HELLO MARY LOU

Words and Music by
GENE PITNEY and
CAYET MANGIARACINA

Edim
Bb
Gm
Cm7
F7-9
Bb
to the ground, And though I nev - er did meet you be - fore.
good an' tight, That's all I had to see for me to stay.
Eb
Bb
F7
Bb7
Eb
I said "hel - lo Ma - ry Lou good - bye
Bb
C9
Am
C7
F7
heart Sweet Ma - ry Lou I'm so in love with you.
Bb
F9
Bb
D7
D+
D7
Gm
C9
C7
knew Ma - ry Lou We'd nev - er part so hel - lo Ma - ry
F7
Dm
F7
1
Bb
F7
2
Bb
Lou good - bye heart." I heart."

GREAT BALLS OF FIRE

Words and Music by
OTIS BLACKWELL and
JACK HAMMER

Bright Rock
C
no chord
You shake my nerves and you rat - tle my brain. _
Instrumental
mf
F7
no chord
Too much love drives a man in - sane. _
G7
no chord
You broke my will,
F7
no chord
but what a thrill.
C
no chord
Good - ness gra - cious, great _ balls of fire!
gliss.
C
I laughed at love 'cause I thought it was fun - ny.
F7
You came a - long and you moved _

G7
F7
me, hon-ey.
I changed my mind,
love's just fine.
C
no chord
F7
Good - ness gra - cious, great balls of fire!
Instrumental ends
Kiss me, ba - by.
Woo,
C
F7
it feels good.
Hold me, ba - by.
G7
Girl, just let me love you like a lov - er should.
I want to love you like a lov - er should.
You're fine,

so kind, __ I'm gon-na tell the world that you're mine, mine, mine, mine. __
C
F7
I chew my nails and I twid - dle my thumb. __ I'm real ner-vous but it
G7
F7
1 C
no chord
sure is fun. __ Come on, ba-by, you're driv-ing me cra - zy. Good - ness gra - cious, great __
2 C
no chord
C
__ balls of fire! Good - ness gra- cious, great __ balls of fire!

HE'S A REBEL

Words and Music by
GENE PITNEY

Moderately fast ♩ = 120
mf
Verse:
F
*
1. See the way he walks down the street. That's the way he shuf-fles his feet.
Dm
B♭
1.
C
How he holds_ his head up high_ when he goes walk-in' by;_ he's my_

*Sing vocal one octave lower.

2.
G7
C
C♯7
guy.
just be-cause of that they say . . .
Chorus:
F♯
D♯m
F♯
f
He's a reb-el and he'll nev-er, ev-er be an-y good. He's a reb-el 'cause he
C♯7
B
nev-er, ev-er does what he should. Well, just be-cause he does-n't do what
A♯
D♯m
ev-'ry-bod-y else does, a-that's no rea-son why

B
G♯7
F♯
I can't give him all my love.
(2nd time only:) we can't share our love.
He is al - ways good to me,
D♯m
B
al - ways treats me ten - der - ly,
(3rd time only:) good to him I'll try to be.
'cause he's not a reb - el, oh, no, no,
C♯7
To Coda
F♯
C♯7
he's not a reb-el, no, no, no, to me.
Solo:
F♯
D♯m
F♯

D♯m
B
C♯7
B
C♯7
D♯m
If they don't like him that way, they
B
G♯7
C♯7
D.S. 𝄋 al Coda
won't like me af - ter to - day, and I'll be stand-ing right by his side when they say . . .
3
3

Coda
F♯
D♯m
me. Oh, he's not a reb - el, no, no, no.
F♯
D♯m
Repeat ad lib. and fade
He's not a reb - el, no, no, no. He's not a reb - el, no, no, no.

Verse 2:
When he holds my hand, I'm so proud,
'Cause he's not just one of the crowd.
My baby's always the one to try the thing they've never done,
And just because of that they say . . .
(To Chorus:)

HOLD ME, THRILL ME, KISS ME

Words and Music by
HARRY NOBLE

Hold Me, Thrill Me, Kiss Me - 3 - 1

Dm7
G7
Am
C+
Am7
Dm7
G7
Hid - ing lov - ers just the same as We'll be, we'll be, when you make me tell you I love
C
Am
Dm7
G7
C
F6
Fm6
you. (Will you take me in your arms.) They told me, "Be sens - i - ble with your
C
C+
C
Dm7
G7
C
new love, Don't be fooled think - ing this is the last you'll find." But
Am6
D7
Em
G+
Em7
they nev - er stood in the dark with you, love, When you

Dm7 G7 C Am6 B7
fooled think - ing this is the last you'll find." But they nev - er stood in the dark with
Em G+ Em7 Am7 D9 Em G7
you, love, When you take me in your arms and drive me slow - ly out of my mind.
C Am7 Dm7 G7 C Am7
Kiss me, kiss me, and when you do, I know that you will Miss me, miss me
Dm7 G7 E7 Am C+ Am7 Dm7 G7
If we ev - er say a-dieu, so Kiss me, kiss me, Make me tell you I'm in love with
1 C Ebdim Dm7 G7 G+7 2 C Am Dm7 G7 C
you. you. (Hold me tight, nev - er let me go.)
rit.

I GOT YOU BABE

Words and Music by
SONNY BONO

F
B♭
E♭
3fr.
C
Gm7
3fr.
C7
you got me, and ba - by, I got you,
F
B♭
F
B♭
babe,
I got you, babe.
I got
F
B♭
F
B♭
you, babe.
They say our love won't pay the rent, Be -
F
B♭
C
Gm7
3fr.
C7
fore it's earned our mon - ey's all been spent.
I

F
B♭
F
E♭
3fr.
guess that's so, we don't have a pot, But at least I'm sure of all the things we
C
Gm7
3fr.
C7
F
B♭
got, babe, I got
F
B♭
F
you, babe I got you, babe. I got
Gm
3fr.
Gm7
3fr.
C7
C7
Gm7
3fr.
C7
flow - ers in the Spring, I got

Gm
3fr.
Gm7
3fr.
C7
C7
Gm7
3fr.
C7
F
you, to wear my ring, And when I'm
F
Gm7
3fr.
sad, you're a clown, And if I get
F
C7
C#7
scared you're al-ways a - round. So
F#
B
F#
E
Let them say your hair's too long, 'cause I don't care, with you I can't do

C♯
G♯m7
4fr.
C♯7
F♯
B
wrong.
Then put your little hand in mine,
F♯
E
C♯
G♯m7
4fr.
C♯7
There ain't no hill or moun - tain we can't climb,
Repeat and fade
F♯
B
F♯
B
babe,
I got
you, babe.
I got

HOW DO YOU DO IT?

Words and Music by
MITCH MURRAY

How Do You Do It? - 2 - 1

B♭ C7 F Dm7 Gm7 C7 F
give me a feel-ing in my heart Like an ar-row passing thro' it
B♭ C7 F Dm7 G7 C G9 C G7
S'pose that you think you're ve-ry smart But won't you tell me How do you do it
C7 F Dm7 Gm7 C7 F Dm7 Gm7 C7
How do you do what you do to me If I on-ly knew Then per-
F Dm7 Gm7 C7 F B♭ F E♭ E F B♭ F B♭ F
1. 2.
haps you'd fall for me like I fell for you. you.

HURT SO BAD

Words and Music by
BOBBY WEINSTEIN, BOBBY HART
and TEDDY RANDAZZO

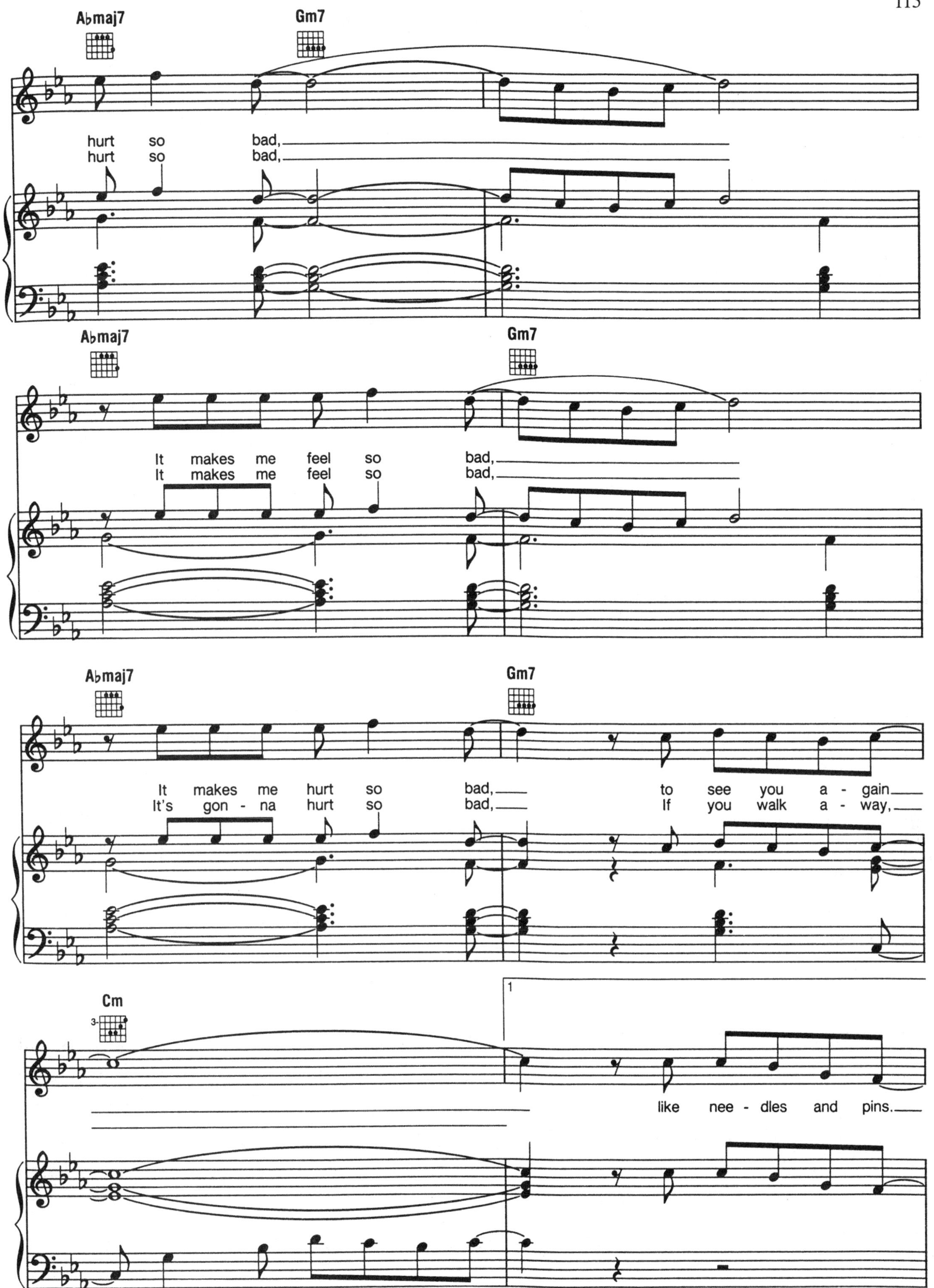
Abmaj7
Gm7
hurt so bad,
hurt so bad,
Abmaj7
Gm7
It makes me feel so bad,
It makes me feel so bad,
Abmaj7
Gm7
It makes me hurt so bad, to see you a - gain
It's gon - na hurt so bad, If you walk a - way,
Cm
1
like nee - dles and pins.

2
Fm7
Peo - ple say why don't you stay
Ab maj7
Gm7
and let me make it up to you.
Ab maj7
Gm7
Cm
Gm7
Stay, I'll do an - y - thing you want me to; You loved me be - fore, please
Ab maj7
Bb7
Ab6
Gm7
Fm7
Bb7
love me a - gain, I can't let you go back to him. Please don't go, please don't

A♭maj7
Gm7
go. It hurts so bad,
f
A♭maj7
Gm7
Come back, it hurts so bad.
A♭maj7
Gm7
Cm
Don't make it hurt so bad, I'm beg-gin' you please.
Fm7
B♭7
E♭
E♭6
Please don't go, please don't go.
rit.

I ONLY WANT TO BE WITH YOU

Words and Music by
MIKE HAWKER and
IVOR RAYMONDE

I Only Want to Be With You - 3 - 1

1.
2.
I on-ly want to be with you. It
I on-ly want to be with you.
D7 D C D Am7 D7 G C D G C G
You stopped and smiled at me, Asked if I'd care to dance.
Eb G C G
I fell in-to your op-en arms and I did-n't stand a chance.
D Bm7 Em7 A7
Now listen honey, I just wanna be beside you ev-ry-where. As long as were to-gether honey
D7 G Em G

I don't care 'Cos you start-ed somethin' Oh can't you see that
Em C D Am7 D7
ev-er since we met you've had a hold on me. No mat - ter what you do,
G Em Am Bm Am C♯dim.
To Coda
D.S. al Coda
I on - ly want to be with you.
D7 D C D Am7 D7 G C G
Coda.
I said I on - ly want to be with you.
rall.
G C G Am7 D7 G C G

IN THE MIDNIGHT HOUR

Words by
WILSON PICKETT

Music by
STEVE CROPPER

A♭
B♭
A♭
hold you, and do all the things I told you in the mid-night
E♭
A♭
E♭
A♭
E♭
A♭
D♭
hour. Yes, I am, oh yes, I am.
B♭
E♭
A♭
E♭
A♭
I'm gon-na wait til stars come out and see that
E♭
A♭
E♭
A♭
E♭
A♭
twin-kle in your eyes, I'm gon-na wait til the mid-night

E♭
A♭
hour, that's when my love be - gins to shine. You'll be the
B♭
A♭ maj7
B♭ 7
on - ly girl I'll love and real - ly love you so in the mid - night
1.
hour, oh yeah, in the mid - night hour. I'm gon - na
2.
hour. I'm gon - na wait til the mid - night hour, I'm gon - na
Repeat and fade

I WANT TO HOLD YOUR HAND

Words and Music by
JOHN LENNON and
PAUL McCARTNEY

Moderately

C D C D C D

f

Oh yeah,

G D Em

I'll ___ tell you some - thing I think you'll un - der -
please ___ say to me ___ you'll let me be your

Bm
G
D
stand. When I ___ say that some - thing,
man, And please ___ say to me ___

Em
Bm
C
D
I want to hold your hand,
you'll let me hold your hand,
I want to hold your
Now let me hold your
G
Em
C
D
1 G
hand,
hand,
I want to hold your hand.
I want to hold your
Oh,
2 G
Dm7
G
hand.
And when I touch you I feel
more smoothly
C
Am
Dm7
hap - py in - side.
It's such a

G
C
D
C
D
feel - ing that my love I can't hide, I can't hide,
C
D
I can't hide!
G
D
Yeah, you got that some - thing
Yeah, you got that some - thing
as before
Em
Bm
G
I think you'll un - der - stand. When I say that
I think you'll un - der - stand. When I feel that

D
Em
Bm
some - thing,
some - thing,
I want to hold your hand,
C
D
G
Em
1 C
D
I want to hold your hand,
I want to hold your
G
2 C
D
B7
hand.
I want to hold your hand,
C
D
C
G
I want to hold your hand.
3
3
3
3

I WILL FOLLOW HIM

(I Will Follow You)

English Words by
NORMAN GIMBEL and ARTHUR ALTMAN
Original Lyric by JACQUES PLANTE

Music by
J.W. STOLE and DEL ROMA

Eb
Cm
Eb
way.
I must fol - low him.
Gm
Ev - er since he touched my hand
I knew
that
Cm
Gm
Ab
near him I al - ways must be,
and noth - ing can keep him from
Bb7
Eb
Bb7
me,
he is my des - tin - y.
I

E♭
Cm
love him, I love him, I love him and where he goes I'll fol-ow,
I'll fol-low, I'll
for - ev - er and
Cm
Fm7
B♭7
E♭
fol-low he'll al-ways be my true love, my true love, my true love, from now un - til for -
ev - er and side by side to - geth - er I'll be with my true love, and share a thou-sand
Cm
no chord
E♭
ev - er, for - ev - er, for - ev - er.
sun-sets to-geth - er be - side him.
I will fol - low him,
Gm
fol-low him wher-ev - er he may go.
There

Cm
Gm
A♭
is - n't an o - cean too deep, a moun - tain so high it can
Fm7
B♭7
E♭
1
E♭/B♭
keep, keep me a - way, a - way from my love.
2
I a - way from my love. Ah

IT'S MY PARTY

Words and Music by
HERB WIENER, JOHN GLUCK
and WALLY GOLD

Moderately bright

f

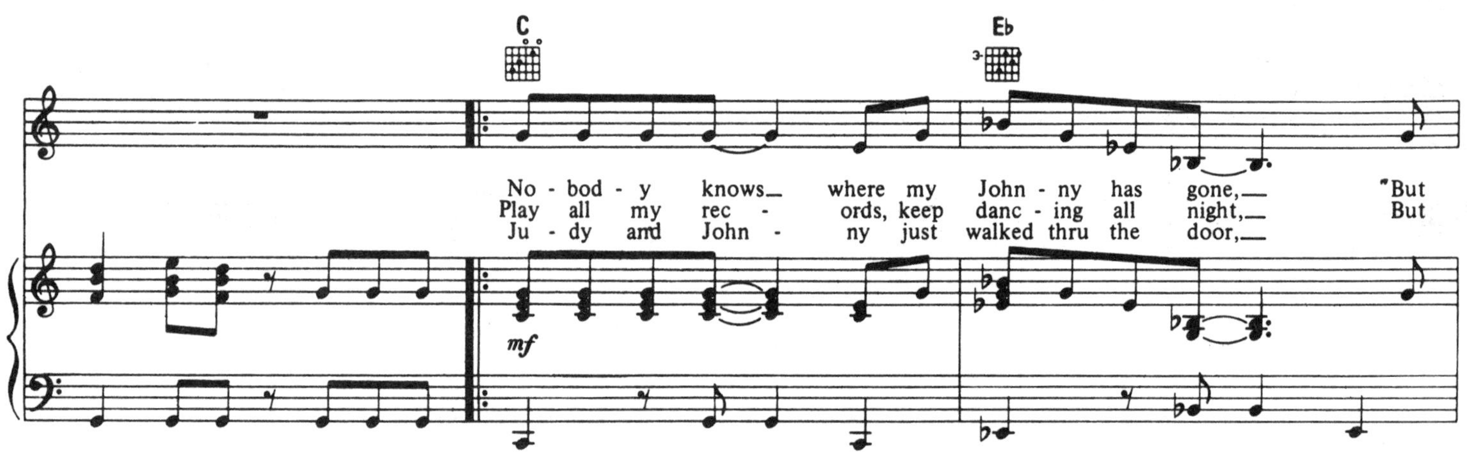
C
Eb
No - bod - y knows where my John - ny has gone, "But
Play all my rec - ords, keep danc - ing all night, But
Ju - dy and John - ny just walked thru the door,
mf

C
F
Ab
Ju - dy left the same time. Why was he
leave me a - lone for a - while, 'Til John - ny's
Like a queen with her king, Oh, what a

C
D7
G7
hold - ing her hand, when he's sup - posed to be mine?
danc - ing with me, I've got no, rea - son to smile.
birth - day sur - prise, Ju - dy's wear - ing his ring.
C
C+
F
It's my par - ty, and I'll cry if I want to, Cry if I want to,
f
Fm
C
G7
Cry if I want to, You would cry, too, if it hap - pened to
C
F
1,2
G7
3
C
you.

ITSY BITSY TEENIE WEENIE YELLOW POLKA DOT BIKINI

Words and Music by
PAUL J. VANCE and LEE POCKRISS

G7
C
G7
That she wore for the first time to - day. An It - sy Bit - sy Tee - nie Wee - nie
C
G7
1.2.
F
C
G7
C
Yel - low Pol - ka - dot Bi - ki - ni, So in the
1. lock - er
2. blan - ket
3. wa - ter
she want - ed to stay. (Two,
3.
F
C
G7
C
three, four, Stick a - round, we'll tell you more.)
2. She was a -
3. Now she's a -
want - ed to stay.
G7
C
From the lock - er to the blan - ket, From the blan - ket to the shore;
G7
C
From the shore to the wa - ter, Guess there is - n't an - y more.
sf

I'VE TOLD EV'RY LITTLE STAR

Words by
OSCAR HAMMERSTEIN II

Music by
JEROME KERN

G7 C Cdim G7
I in love? I al - ways an - swer "Yes," Might as well con -
Am Dm7 G7 C7 F
fess, If I don't, they guess. May - be
Gm7 C11 B♭m/Fbass Fmaj7 F♯dim Gm7 B♭m6 F A♭dim
you may know it too, oh, my dar - ling, if you do, Why have - n't
Gm7 C7-9 F No chord F
you told me?

KEEP A-KNOCKIN'

Words and Music by
RICHARD PENNIMAN

G
Come back to - mor - row night and try it a - gain.
You said you loved me but you can't come in.
You said you loved me but you can't come in.
D7
You said you loved me but you can't come in.

G
Come back to - mor - row night and try it a - gain.
D7
G
1,2
3

LIGHTNIN' STRIKES

Words and Music by
LOU CHRISTIE and TWYLA HERBERT

Moderately
Eb
Eb7
Fm/Eb
Eb
mf
Eb7
Fm/Eb
Eb
Eb7
Fm/Eb
Lis - ten to me, ba - by, you got - ta un - der - stand.
Eb
Eb7
Fm/Eb
You're old e - nough to know the mak - ings of a man.
Eb
Eb7
Fm/Eb
Lis - ten to me, ba - by, it's hard to set - tle down;

E♭
E♭7
Fm/E♭
am I ask - ing too much for you to stick a - round?
C
Dm
G7
Ev - 'ry boy wants a girl he can trust to the
When I set - tle down I want one ba - by
C
Dm
ve - ry end. Ba - by, that's you, won't you
on my mind. For - give and for - get and I'll
G7
C
wait? But till then, when I see lips beg - gin'
make up for all lost time if she's put to - geth - er fine, if she's

to be kissed,
read-ing my mind,
I can't stop!
I can't stop 'cause that
Fm7
Gm7
light - ning's strik - ing a - gain.
C9
Fm7
Light - ning's strik - ing a -
Gm7
To Coda
C9
1Eb
gain!
Na-ture's tak-ing o-ver my

E♭7
Fm/E♭
E♭
one track mind. I need ya. I want ya in my
heart all the time. All the girls are say-ing that you'll end up a fool.
For the time be-ing, ba-by, live by the rule!
2
C
Dm
G7
There's a chap-el in the pines wait-ing for us a-

C
Dm
round the bend. Pic - ture in ___ your mind love for -
G7
C
ev - er, but till then if she give me a sign that she
D.S. al Coda
CODA
C9
Fm7
wants to make time ___ Light - ning's
Gm7
C9
Repeat and Fade
strik - ing a - gain! ___

LET THE GOOD TIMES ROLL

Words and Music by
LEONARD LEE

B♭
F
C7
1. F
2. F
Come on, baby, LET THE GOOD TIMES ROLL,
Roll on and on.
on.
B♭
F
C7
F
B♭
Feel so good in my arms, Sugar
Opt. Feel so good when you're close, Sugar
F
G7
(opt.)
C7
F
baby, you're my good luck charm.
baby, I dig you the most.
Come on, baby, LET THE GOOD TIMES ROLL,
Come on, baby, let me thrill your soul;
B♭
F
Come on, baby, LET THE GOOD TIMES ROLL,
C7
1. F
D.S.
2. F
Roll on and on.
on.
D.S.

LET'S TWIST AGAIN

Words and Music by
DAVE APPELL and KAL MANN

C7
F
C
Ee - ah 'roun' 'n a 'roun' 'n a up 'n down we go a -
F
F#
G7
gain. Oh ba - by, make me know you love me so, an'
C
Am
then let's twist a - gain, like we did last sum - mer.
F
G
C
Yeah, let's twist a - gain, like we did last year.

MACK THE KNIFE

English Words by
MARC BLITZSTEIN
Original German Words by
BERT BRECHT

Music by
KURT WEILL

Moderately, with a beat
C6
Am7
Dm7
mf
G7
G9
C6
Oh, the shark has pret - ty
Dm
Dm7
G9
teeth, dear and he shows them
C6
C
Am
pearl - y white. Just a jack - knife

Am7
Dm7
has Mac - heath, dear and he
G7
C6
G9
keeps it out of sight. When the
C6
Dm
shark bites with his teeth, dear
Dm7
G9
C6
scar - let bil - lows start to spread.

C
Am
Am7
Fan - cy gloves, though wears Mac -
Dm7
heath, dear so there's not a
G7
C6
G9
trace of red. On the
C6
Dm
side - walk Sun - day morn - ing
Mil - ler dis - ap - peared, dear

Dm7
G9
C6
lies a bod - y ooz - ing life;
af - ter draw - ing out his cash;
Am
Am7
Dm7
some one's sneak - ing 'round the cor - ner.
and Mac - heath spends like a sail - or.
G7
C6
Is the some - one Mack the knife?
Did our boy do some - thing rash?
G9
C6
Dm
From a tug - boat by the riv - er
Su - key Taw - dry Jen - ny Div - er

Dm7
G9
A ce - ment bag's drop - ping
Pol - ly Peach - um Lu - cy
C6
Am
Am7
down; The ce - ment's just for the
Brown oh, the line forms on the
Dm7
G7
weight, dear. Bet you Mack - ie's back in
right, dear now that Mack - ie's back in
1 C6
G9
2 C6
town. Lou - ie
town.
rall.

MOCKINGBIRD

Words and Music by
INEZ FOXX and CHARLIE FOXX
Additional Lyrics by JAMES TAYLOR

Moderate beat
p
F
C7
Ev - er - y - bod - y have you heard? He's gon - na buy me a mock-ing - bird,
mf
And if that mock - ing - bird won't sing, he's gon - na buy
F
Bb
me a dia - mond ring, And if that dia - mond ring won't shine,

F
C7
he's gon-na sure-ly break this heart of mine,
And that's why I keep on
Bb7
C7
Tacet
F
tell-in' ev-'ry-bod-y, say-in' wo, wo, wo, wo, wo.
Hear me now and un-der-stand
C7
he's gon-na find me some peace of mind.
And if that peace of mind won't stay,
F
F7
I'm gon-na find my-self a bet-ter way.
And if that

Well, now, everybody have you heard?
She's gonna buy me a mocking bird
If that mocking bird don't sing,
She's gonna buy me a diamond ring.
And if that diamond ring won't shine
Guess it surely break this poor heart of mine,
And that's the reason why I keep on tellin' everybody sayin'
No, no, no, no, no, no, no, no.

Listen now and understand
She's gonna find me some peace of mind.
And if that peace of mind won't stay,
I'm gonna get myself a better way
I might rise above, I might go below,
Ride with the tide and go with the flow,
And that's the reason why I keep on shouting in your ears, y'all
No, no, no, no, no, no, now, now, baby.

MR. LEE

Words and Music by
HEATHER DIXON, HELEN GATHERS,
JANICE POUGHT, EMMA RUTH POUGHT
and LAURA WEBB

F
Dm
Gm7
3 fr
C7
Lee, Mis - ter Lee, Oh! Mis - ter Lee, Mis - ter Lee, Mis - ter Lee, Oh!
Mis - ter Lee, Mis - ter Lee, Mis - ter Lee, Oh!
To Coda
N.C.
Mis - ter Lee, Mis - ter Lee.
I met my
Here comes Mis - ter
sweet - ie his name is Mis - ter Lee.
Lee, he's com - in' for me.

Bb7
I met my sweet - ie his name is Mis - ter
Here comes Mis - ter Lee he's com - in' for
F
C7
Lee. He's the hand - som-est sweet - ie
me. He's my lov - er boy
Gm7/C
C7
F
N.C.
that you ev - er did see. My heart is
let's jump for joy. Come on Mis - ter
F
ach - in' for you Mis - ter Lee.
Lee and do your stuff.

B♭7
My heart is ach - in' for you Mis - ter
Come on, Mis - ter Lee, and do your
F
C7
Lee. 'Cause I love you so
stuff. 'Cause you're gon - na be mine
Gm9
C7
F
1
and I'll nev - er let you go. Mis - ter
till the end of time.
2
D.S. al Coda
CODA
F
Lee.
8vb

MRS. BROWN YOU'VE GOT A LOVELY DAUGHTER

Words and Music by
TREVOR PEACOCK

Shuffle beat

mf

C Em7

Mis - sis Brown you've
She wants to re -

Dm7 G7 C Em7 Dm7 G7 C Em7

got a love - ly daugh - ter,
turn those things I bought her,

Girls as sharp as
Tell her she can

Dm7 G7 C Em7 Dm7 G7 Am C

her are some - thing rare;
keep them just the same;

But it's sad,
Things have changed,

Am C Am C Em

She does - n't love me now, She's made it clear e - nough, It

C
G7
G7
Bb7
ain't no good to pine.
pine.
E
Gm
Ab
Bb
Walk - in' a - bout,
E - ven in a crowd, well,
Gb
Bbm
Bb
G7
You'd pick 'er out,
Made a bloke feel so proud.
C
Em7
Dm7
G7
C
Em7
Dm7
G7
If she finds that I've been 'round to see you,

C
Em7
Dm7
G7
Tell her that I'm well and feel - in' fine;
Am
Don't let on,
Don't say she's broke my heart,
Em
I'd go down on my knees, but it's no good to pine.
Mis - sis Brown you've got a love - ly daugh - ter.
Repeat and Fade

PAPA'S GOT A BRAND NEW BAG

Words and Music by
JAMES BROWN

C/G
D7
C6
no chord
He ain't no drag.
Pa-pa's got a brand new
D7
bag.
1
Come here
2
He's do-ing the
G6
Jerk.
He's do-ing the Fly.
Don't play him cheap 'cause you know he ain't
shy.
He's do-ing the Mon-key,
the Mashed Po-

ta - toes, Jump back Jack, See you la - ter al - li - ga - tor. Come here
sis - ter, Pa - pa's in the swing.
C/G
C9
He ain't too hip now but I can dig that new breed
G6
C/G
D7
babe. He ain't no drag.

C6
no chord
D7
He's got a brand new bag. Oh,
G6
Pa - pa, he's do-ing the Jerk. Pa - pa, he's do-ing the
C9
Jerk. He's do-ing the Twist just like this. He's do - ing the
G6
D7
Fly ev-'ry day and ev-'ry night. The thing's

C6
no chord
D7
like the Boom - er - ang.
Hey, come
G6
on. Hey! Hey, come on. Hey!
Hey, he's up tight, out of sight, come
on. Hey! Hey!

NA NA HEY HEY KISS HIM GOODBYE

Words and Music by
GARY DE CARLO, DALE FRASHUER and PAUL LEKA

Bb
A7
Dm7
G7
He might be thrill - ing ba - by, but, my love's so dog - gone will - ing so
F
Bb
Bbm
C6
F
kiss him, go on and kiss him good - bye. Na na
Ab
1
Eb
F
C7
2
Eb
F
C7
na na, Hey hey, hey, good - bye. Na na hey, hey good - bye. Na na
Repeat and Fade
F
Ab
Eb
F
C7
na na na na na na, Hey hey hey, good - bye. Na na

OUR DAY WILL COME

Words and Music by
MORT GARSON and BOB HILLIARD

Slowly, with expression

mf

G Bb7 Am7 D7

mp

Our Day Will Come and we'll have ev - 'ry-thing.

G Bb7 Am7 D7 Dm7 G7

We'll share the joy fall - ing in love can bring. No one can

Dm7 G7 Cmaj7 C6 Cm7

tell me that I'm too young to know, I love you so and you love

Bm7
Bb7
Am7
D7
G
Bb7
Am7
me.
Our Day Will Come
if we just
D7
G
Bb7
Am7
D7
wait a-while.
No tears for us,
think love and wear a smile.
Dm7
G7
Dm7
G7
Cmaj7
Cm7
G
Em7
Our dreams have mag - ic be- cause we'll al - ways stay in love this way, Our Day
Am7
D7
G
Am7
D7
G
Will Come.
Come.

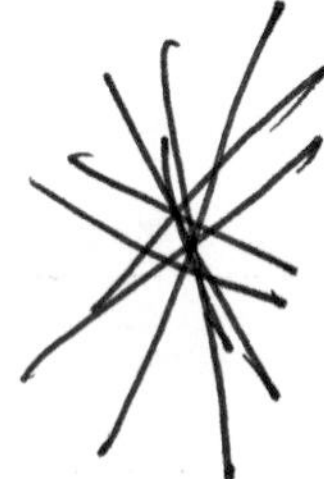

PLEASE, PLEASE ME

Words and Music by
JOHN LENNON and PAUL McCARTNEY

With a beat

G
Bb
C
D7
3
Last night I said these words to my girl
You don't need me to show the way love
3

G
3
I know you nev - er e - ven try girl
Why do I al - ways have to say love
Come
3

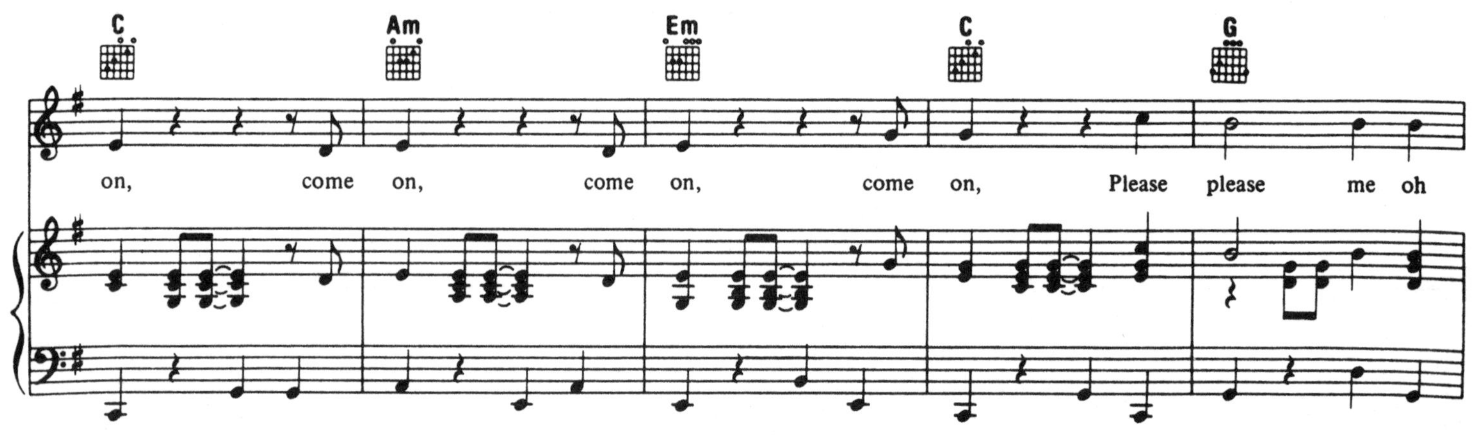
C
Am
Em
C
G
on, come on, come on, come on, Please please me oh

C
D7
G
1
D7
2
G
Yeh like I please you.
C
D7
G
3
I don't want to sound com - plain - ing But you know there's al - ways rain in my heart.
3
C
D7
I do all the pleas - ing with you It's so hard to rea - son with
G
C
D7
G
you. Oh yeh why do you make me blue.

G Bb C D7

Last night I said these words to my ___ girl,

G C

I know you nev - er e - ven try ___ girl Come on, come

Am Em C G C D7

on, come on, come on Please please me oh yeh like I please

1 G D7 2 G

you. you. ___

REBEL 'ROUSER

By
DUANE EDDY
and LEE HAZLEWOOD

B♭
F
C7#5
F
C7
C7#5
F
C7#5
F

B♭
F
C7#5
F
C7sus
C7#5
1 F
C7#5
2 F
B♭7
F

POETRY IN MOTION

Words and Music by
MIKE ANTHONY and
PAUL KAUFMAN

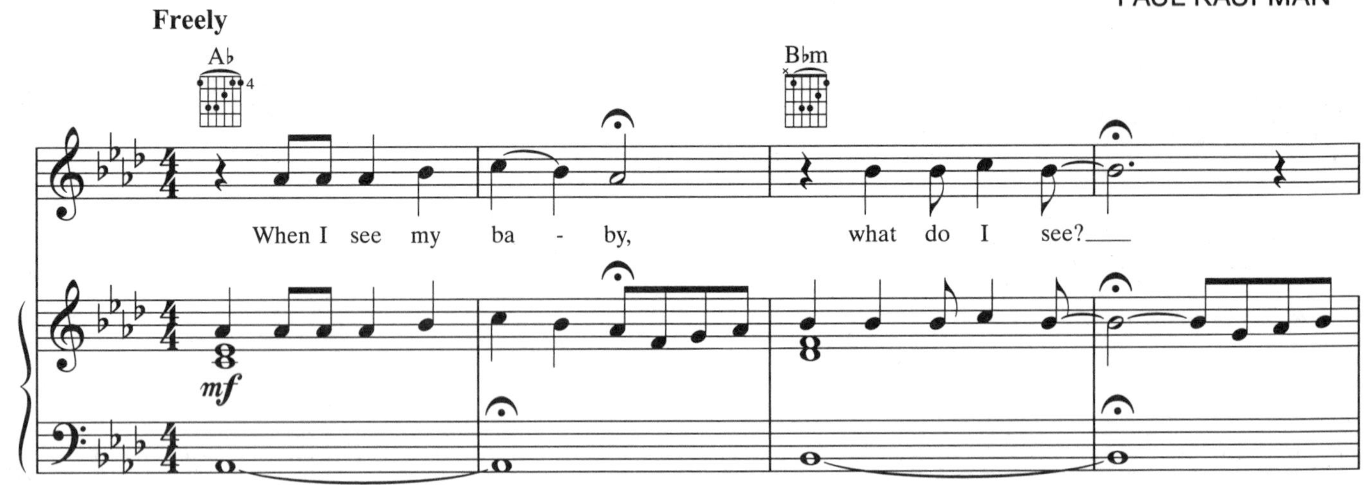
Freely
A♭
B♭m
When I see my ba - by,
what do I see?
mf

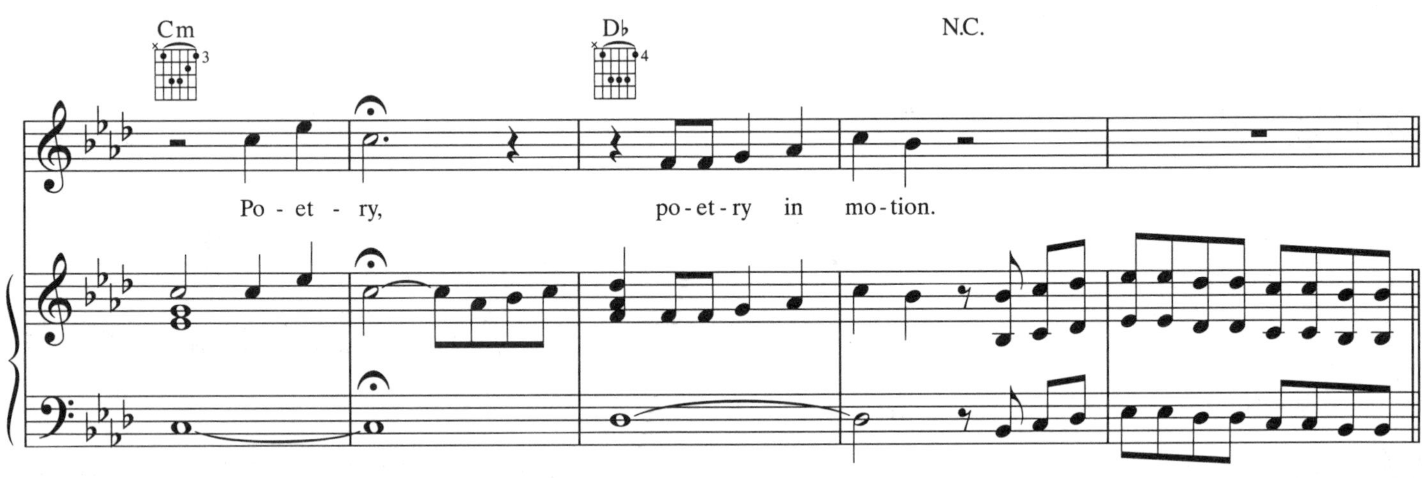
Cm
D♭
N.C.
Po - et - ry,
po - et - ry in mo - tion.

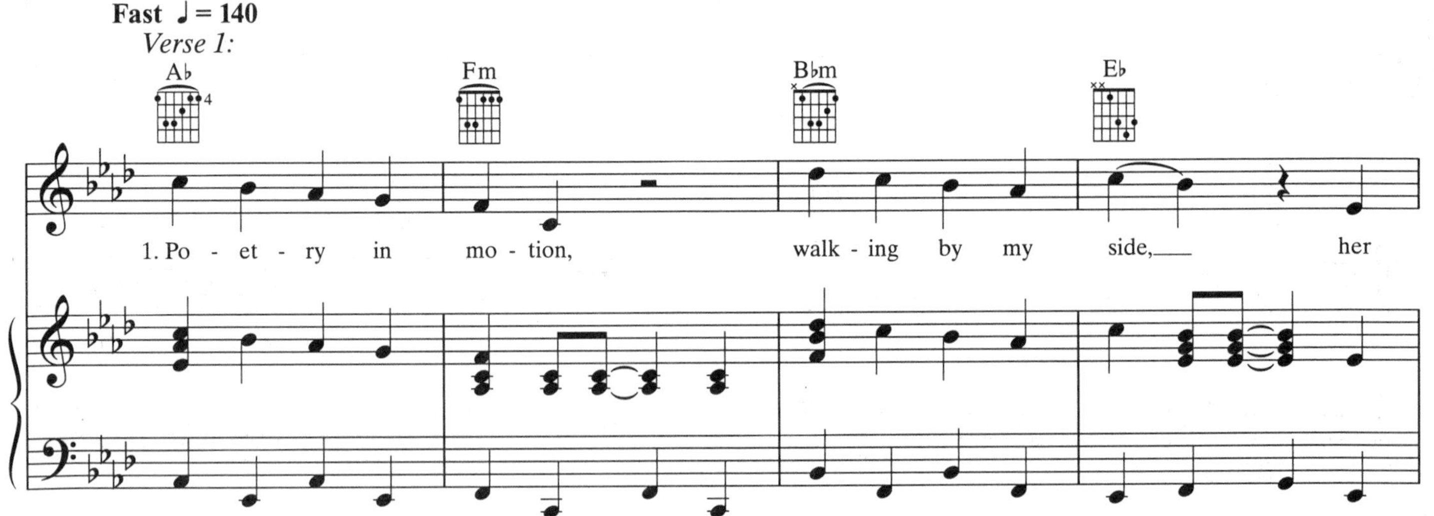
Fast ♩ = 140
Verse 1:
A♭
Fm
B♭m
E♭
1. Po - et - ry in mo - tion,
walk - ing by my side,
her

A♭
Fm
B♭m
E♭
love - ly lo - co - mo - tion, keeps my eyes o - pen wide.
Verses 2 & 4:
A♭
Fm
B♭m
E♭
2.4. Po - et - ry in mo - tion, see her gen - tle sway, a
A♭
Fm
B♭m
E♭
wave out in the o - cean, could nev - er move that
Bridge:
A♭
C
Fm
way. I love ev - 'ry move - ment. There's

C
Fm
C
noth - ing I would change. She does - n't need_ im - prove -
D♭
B♭m
E♭
ment, she's much too nice to re - ar - range.
Verses 3 & 5:
A♭
Fm
B♭m
E♭
3. Po - et - ry in mo - tion, danc - ing close to me, a
5. Po - et - ry in mo - tion, all that I a - dore, no
A♭
Fm
B♭m
E♭
A♭
flow - er of de - vo - tion, for all the world to see.
num - ber nine love po - tion could make me love her more.

A♭
Fm
B♭m
Whoa, oh whoa whoa whoa whoa whoa, oh
E♭
A♭
Fm
B♭m
whoa whoa whoa whoa whoa, oh whoa whoa whoa whoa whoa, oh
1.
2.
E♭
E♭
A♭
whoa. whoa whoa whoa whoa whoa, oh
Fm
B♭m
E♭
Repeat ad lib. and fade
whoa whoa whoa whoa whoa, oh whoa whoa whoa whoa

PRIMROSE LANE

Words and Music by
WAYNE SHANKLIN and
GEORGE CALLENDER

Am Am7 D7 G G7 C
in the rain with you. Sweet per - fume!
mf
G7 C G7 G#dim Am E+
Those lit - tle ol' ros - es bloom And I wan - na walk with you
Am7 Am F7 D7 G
My whole life through. Prim-rose Lane,
mp
G#dim Am Am7
Life's a hol - i - day on Prim-rose Lane, Just a hol - i - day on Prim-rose Lane
D7 G D7 G
with you. you.
f

RHYTHM OF THE RAIN

Words and Music by
JOHN GUMMOE

Moderate rock

F Bb F C7

Lis-ten to the rhy-thm of the fall - ing rain,_ tell-ing me just what a fool I've been. I

mf

F Bb F Gm7 C7 F

wish that it would go and let me cry in vain_ and let me be a - lone a - gain._ The

F Bb F C7

on - ly girl I care a - bout has gone a - way_ look-in' for a brand-new start._ But

F
Bb
F
Gm7
C7
F
lit-tle does she know that when she left that day_ a- long with her she took my heart._
Bb
Am
Bb
Rain, please tell me now does that seem fair,_ For her to steal my heart a-way when
Rain, won't you tell her that I love her so,_ please ask the sun to set my
F
Dm
Gm7
C7
F
she don't care._ I can't love an-oth-er when my heart's some-where_ far a- way.
heart a - glow._ Rain in her heart and let the love we knew_ start to grow.
1.
C7
2.
C7
D. S.
al Coda
Coda
F
F
Dm
The
Lis-ten to the rhy-thm of the fall-ing rain,_

(WE'RE GONNA) ROCK AROUND THE CLOCK

Words and Music by
MAX C. FREEDMAN and JIMMY DE KNIGHT

Rock beat
Verse:
Fm
C7+
C7
One, two, three o' - clock, Four o' - clock, Rock.
Five, six sev - en o' - clock, Eight o' - clock, Rock. Nine, ten, e - lev - en o' - clock,
Bb7
C11
F
Twelve o' - clock, Rock. We're Gon - na Rock A - round The Clock to - night.

Chorus:
F
1. Put your glad rags on and join me, hon, We'll
2. (When the) clock strikes two and three and four, If the
3. (When the) chimes ring five and six and sev - en, We'll be
4. (When it's) eight, nine, ten, e - lev - en, too, I'll be
5. (When the) clock strikes twelve, we'll cool off, Then start - a
f
F7
have some fun when the clock strikes one,
band slows down, we'll yell for more,
rock - in' up in sev - enth heav'n,
go - ing strong and so will you,
rock - in' 'round the clock a - gain,
We're Gon - na
Bb9
F
Rock A - round The Clock to - night, We're gon - na rock, rock, rock 'til

1.2.3.4.
G7
C11
C7+
C11
F6
broad day - light, We're gon - na rock, gon - na rock a - round the clock to - night!
5. G7
C11
2.3.5. When the rock, gon - na rock a - round
4. When it's
C7+
C11
F6
the clock to - night!
3
ff

ROSES ARE RED

(My Love)

Words anc
AL BYRON anc

Moderately
mf
G7
C
F
C7
mp
1. A long, long time a - go on grad - u - a - tion day You hand - ed me your book, I signed this way:
through high school and when the big day came, I wrote in - to your book next to my name:
lit - tle girl? She looks a lot like you. Some - day some boy will write in her book, too:
ROS - ES ARE RED, my love,

C
Am
Vi - 'lets are blue, Sug - ar is
F
G7
1C
sweet my love, But not as sweet as you. 2. We da - ted
mp
2C
To Next Strain
3 C
F
C
G7
C
Fine
you.
you.
molto rit.
p
F
G
G7
C
Then I went far a - way and you found some - one

C7
F
G7
C
F7
new. I read your let - ter, dear, and I wrote back to
G7
C7
F
you: ROS - ES ARE RED, my love, Vi-'lets are
C
Am
F
blue, Sug - ar is sweet, my love Good
G7
C
D.S. al Fine
luck, may God bless you. 3. Is that your
mp

RUNAROUND SUE

Words and Music by
DION DI MUCCI and
ERNIE MARESCA

2.
A
D
hayp. Ah
I should have known it from the ve - ry start,
I miss her lips and the smile on her face, the
Bm
G
this girl will leave me with a bro - ken heart.
touch of her hair and this girl's warm em - brace.
Now lis - ten peo - ple what I'm
So if you don't wan - na cry
A
N.C.
tell - ing you
like I do
a - keep a - way from a Run - a - round Sue.
D
Bm
Hayp hayp bum - da ha - dy ha - dy, hayp hayp bum - da ha - dy ha - dy,
(Oh, oh, oh, oh,

G
A
hayp hayp bum-da ha-dy ha-dy hayp. Ah
oh, oh.)
G
D
She likes to trav-el a-round,
she'll love you but she'll put you down.
G
A
N.C.
Now peo-ple let me put you wise,
Sue goes
D
out with oth-er guys. Here's the mor-al and the sto-ry from the guy who knows,

Bm
I fell in love and my love___ still grows.__
G
Ask an - y fool that
she ev - er knew__ they'll say
A
N.C.
keep a - way from - a Run - a - round Sue.
D
Hayp hayp
bum - da ha - dy ha - dy,
Bm
hayp hayp
(Fade after D.S.)
bum - da ha - dy ha - dy,
G
hayp hayp
bum - da ha - dy ha - dy
A
N.C.
hayp.
Ah
D.S. al fade

SAVE YOUR HEART FOR ME

Words by
PETER UDELL

Music by
GARY GELD

Eb
Ab
G7
Cm
Ab
1
Eb/Bb
but re-mem - ber I'm in love with you. And save your heart for
Please don't let the stars get in your eyes. Just
Bb7sus
Bb7
2
Eb/Bb
Bb7
Eb
me!
save your heart __ for me!
Cm
Gm
Ab
When you're all a-lone, far a-way from home; some-one's gon - na flirt with
Eb
Cm
Gm
you! ___
I won't think it's wrong if you play a-long,

A♭
Fm7
B♭7sus
B♭7
E♭
just don't fall for some - one new. When the au - tumn winds be -
mf
Gm
Fm
A♭m
gin to blow, and the sum - mer-time is long a - go;
E♭
A♭
G7
Cm
A♭
E♭
E♭7
you'll be in my arms a - gain, I know. So, save your heart for
A♭6
A♭m
E♭/B♭
Cm
A♭maj7
B♭7
me, dar - lin', save your heart for

Eb
Gm
Fm
Abm
(Whistle)
me.
Eb
Ab
G7
Cm
Ab
Please re - mem ber I'm in love with you, and
Eb
Eb7
Ab6
Abm
Eb/Bb
Cm
save your heart for me, dar - lin', save your
Abmaj7
Bb7
Eb
heart for me.

SEA CRUISE

Words and Music by
HUEY SMITH

Moderately
mf
C
G7
1. Old man rhy - thm is in my shoes, It's no use sit - tin' and sing - in' the blues, So be my guest you got noth - in' to lose,
2. got to get to rock-in' get my hat off the rack, You know the boog - ie woog - ie hit me right in the back, So be my guest you got noth - in' to lose,
3. got to get to mov - in', ba - by, I ain't liein', My heart's beat - in' rhy - thm and it's right on time, Now be my guest you got noth - in' to lose,
Won't

C
you let me take you on a SEA CRUISE. Ooh wee, Ooh
C
wee ba - by, Ooh wee, Ooh
C
G7
wee ba - by, Ooh wee, Ooh
G7
C
wee ba - by, Won't you let me take you on a

C
F
SEA CRUISE. Feel like trav - 'lin', Ba -
F
C
- by won't ya join me please,
C
F
I don't like beg - gin', But now
F
G7
(Third time D. S. 𝄋 and fade)
I'm on bend - in' knees.
2. I
3. I

SHAKE RATTLE AND ROLL

Words and Music by
CHARLES CALHOUN

Cdim
Dm7
G9
C6
Well, roll my break - fast, 'cause I'm a hun - gry man.
CHORUS
C6
Shake Rat - tle and Roll,
Shake rat - tle and roll,
C7
F9
C6
Shake rat - tle and roll,
Shake rat - tle and roll;
Cdim
Dm7
G7
You nev - er do noth - in' to save your dog - gone

1
C6
to 2nd Verse
soul.
2
C6
to 3rd Verse
soul.
3
C6
Fine
soul.
Verse 2
C6
Wear - in' those dress - es, your hair done up so right,
C7
F9
Wear - in' those dress - es, your
C6
Cdim
hair done up so right;
You

Dm7
G9
C6
D.S. 2nd ending
look so warm, but your heart is cold as ice.
Verse 3
C6
I'm like a one - eyed cat,
peep - in' in a sea - food store,
C7
F9
I'm like a one - eyed cat,
C6
Cdim
Dm7
peep - in' in a sea - food store;
I can look at you, tell you

C7
C6
Verse 4
C6
don't love me no more.
I be -
C7
lieve you're do - in' me wrong _ and now I know, _
I be -
F9
C6
Cdim
lieve you're do - in' me wrong _ and now I know; _
The
Dm7
G7
C6
D.S. al Fine
(3rd ending)
more I work, the fast - er my mon - ey goes.

SEALED WITH A KISS

Words by
PETER UDELL

Music by
GARY GELD

Sealed With a Kiss - 2 - 1

Dm Gm Dm G Dm G
Kiss. I'll see you in the sun-light, I'll hear your voice ev-'ry-
Dm G Dm E7
where. I'll run to ten-der-ly hold you, But, dar-ling, you won't be
A7 (Tacit) G Gm Dm Gm C
there. I don't wan-na say good-bye for the sum-mer, Know-ing the love we'll
F D+ Gm C Dm Gm6 C
miss. Oh, let us make a pledge to meet in Sep-tem-ber, And seal it with a
fzp
1. Dm Gm6 A7 (Tacit) 2. Dm Gm A7 Dm
kiss. 'Tho we got-ta say good- kiss.
fz
rit.

SHE'S NOT THERE

Words and Music by
ROD ARGENT

Bridge:
Am
F
A
D/F♯
F
how man-y peo - ple cried.
though they all knew.
1.2. But it's too (3.) late to say you're
cresc.
mf
Am
Em7
Am
D/F♯
F
sor-ry; how would I know? Why should I care? Please don't both - er try'n' to find
C
E7
her; she's not there.
Well, let me tell you 'bout the
cresc.
Chorus:
Am
D
Am
F
Am
D
way she looked, the way she act - ed, the col-or of her hair; her voice was
ff

Am
F
Am
D
A
soft and cool, her eyes were clear and bright, but she's not there.
1.
2.
To Next Strain
3.
Fine
N.C.
N.C.
N.C.
Am
D6
mp
f
(Inst. solo ad lib....
Am7
D6
Am
D6
Am7
D6
Am
D6
Am7
D6
Am
D6
A
D.S. 𝄋 al Fine
...end solo) 3. But it's too

SINCE I MET YOU BABY

Words and Music by
IVORY JOE HUNTER

Slow Blues

Refrain

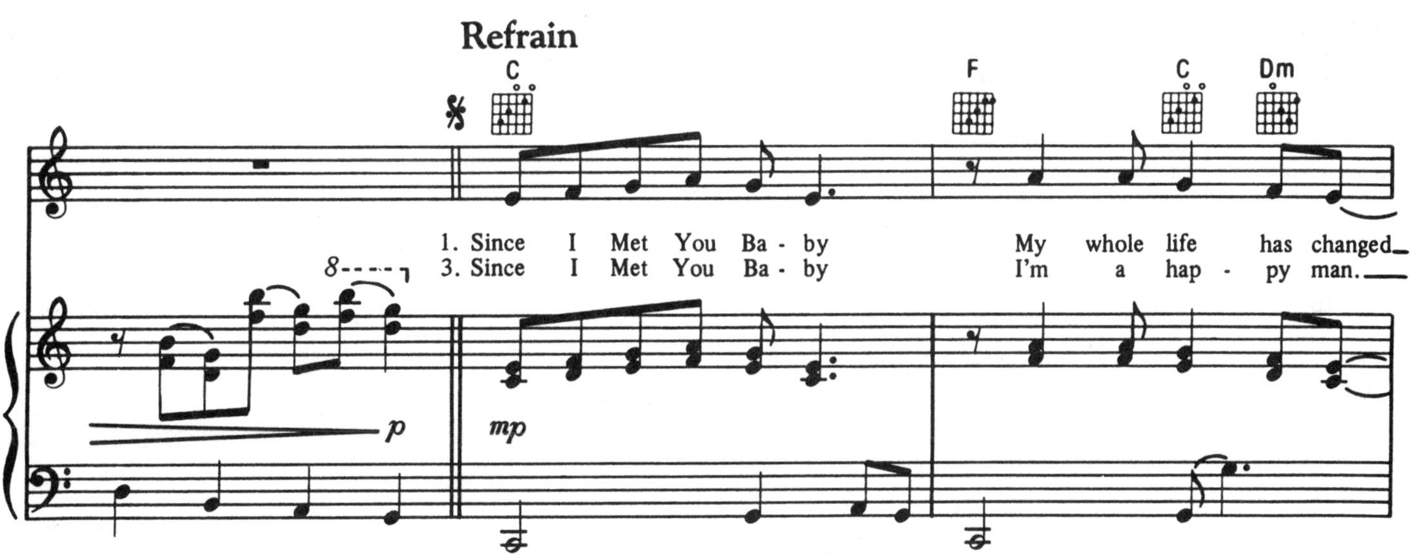

C
C7
F
Since I Met You Ba - by
Since I Met You Ba - by
C
My whole life has changed.
I'm a hap py - man.
And
I'm
G7
1 C
ev - 'ry - bod - y tells me that I am not the same.
gon- na try to please you in ev - 'ry way I
G7
To 2nd Refrain
2 C
G7
C
Fine
can.
p
mf

Refrain
C
F
C
Dm
C
2. I don't need no - bod - y to tell my trou - bles to,
mp
8
C7
F
I don't need no - bod - y to tell my trou - bles to,
C
G7
'Cause Since I Met You Ba - by
all I need is you.
D.S. al Fine
p

SH-BOOM
(Life Could Be A Dream)

Words and Music by
JAMES KEYES, CLAUDE FEASTER,
CARL FEASTER, FLOYD McRAE and JAMES EDWARDS

Moderately bright
Eb
Cm
Hey non - ny ding dong a -
mp

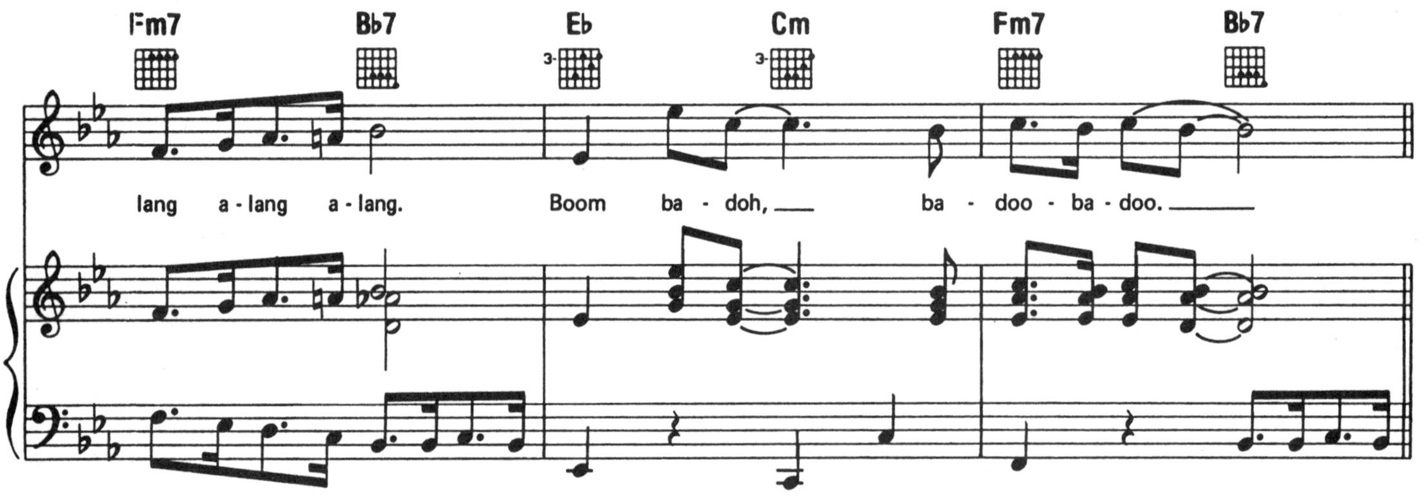
Fm7
Bb7
Eb
Cm
Fm7
Bb7
lang a - lang a - lang. Boom ba - doh, ba - doo - ba - doo.

Eb
Cm
Fm7
Bb7
Eb
Cm
Life could be a dream, sh - boom, if I could take you up in Par - a - dise up a - bove, sh -
mf
3

Fm7 Bb7 Eb Cm Fm7 Bb7
boom. If you would tell me I'm the on - ly one that you love, life could be a dream, sweet-
Eb Cm Fm7 Bb7 Eb Cm
heart. Hel - lo, hel - lo a - gain, sh - boom, and hop - in' we'll meet a - gain. Oh, life could be a dream, sh -
Fm Bb7 Eb Cm Fm7 Bb7
boom, if on - ly all my pre - cious plans would come true, sh - boom. If you would let me spend my
Eb Cm Fm7 Bb7 Eb Ab7 Eb Ab7
whole life lov - in' you, life could be a dream, sweet - heart.

G7
C7
Ev - 'ry time I look at you some - thing is on my mind.
F7
Fm7
Bb7
If you'd do what I want you to, ba - by, we'd be so fine. Oh,
Eb
Cm
Fm7
Bb7
Eb
Cm
life could be a dream, sh - boom, if I could take you up in Par - a - dise up a - bove, sh -
Fm7
Bb7
Eb
Cm
Fm7
Bb7
To Coda
boom. If you would tell me I'm the on - ly one that you love, life could be a dream, sweet -

1
Eb
Cm
Fm7
Bb7
2 Eb
heart.
Sh -
boom sh - boom, ya da da da da da da da da da. Sh - boom sh - boom, ya da da da da da da da da da. Sh-
1 Eb
Guitar Tacet
boom sh - boom, ya da da da da da da da da da, sh - boom.
2
D.S. al Coda
CODA
boom.
heart.

SMOKE GETS IN YOUR EYES

Lyrics by
OTTO HARBACH

Music by
JEROME KERN

E♭
B♭7
E♭
-nied."
They said some-day you'll
B♭7(sus)
B♭7
E♭
E♭+
A♭
E♭dim
find, All who love are blind.
When your heart's on
accel.
E♭
Fmi7
B♭7
E♭
fire, You must re-al-ize Smoke gets in your eyes.
a tempo
B
Un poco più mosso
F♯7
F♯dim
So I chaffed them and I gay-ly laughed, to think they could doubt my
mf

F♯7
B
Abmi7
Bb7
love. Yet to-day, My love has flown a-way, I am with-
Eb
Bb7
Eb
out my love. Now laugh-ing friends de-
p
poco rit.
p a tempo
Bb7(sus)
Bb7
Eb
Eb+
Ab
Ebdim
ride, Tears I can-not hide, So I smile and
poco accel.
Eb
Fmi7
Bb7
Eb
say, "When a love-ly flame dies. Smoke gets in your eyes."
allarg.

STAGGER LEE

Words and Music by
HAROLD LOGAN and
LLOYD PRICE

F7
Bb6
F7
F7+5
gam - bling in the dark. It was
brand new Stet-son hat. Stag-ger
pulled his for - ty four. Stag-ger
Bb
F7
Bb7
Eb7
Stag-ger Lee and Bil - ly, Two men who gam-ble
Lee went home, And he got his for - ty
Lee cried Bil - ly, "Oh please don't take my
Bb
F7
late, Stag-ger Lee threw sev - en, Bil - ly swore that he threw
four, Said "I'm go - ing to the bar-room just to pay that debt I
life, I got three lit - tle child-ren and a ver - y sick - ly
1. 2.
8.
Bb6
F7
F7+5
Bb6
F7
F7+5
eight. 2. Stag-ger wife. 4. Stag-ger
owe. 3. Stag-ger

Bb
F7+5
Bb7
Eb7
Lee shot Bil-ly, Oh, he shot that poor boy so bad, 'Till the
F7
bul-let came through Bil-ly, and it broke the bar - ten-der's glass. Look out now Go,
go, Stag-ger Lee. Go, go, Stag-ger Lee. Go, go, Stag-ger Lee. Go, go, Stag-ger Lee. Go,
Bb6
go, Stag-ger Lee. Go, go, Stag-ger Lee. Go, go, Stag-ger Lee. Go, go!
sfz

STOP STOP STOP

Words and Music by
TONY HICKS, GRAHAM NASH and ALLAN CLARKE

Moderately bright 2
mf
E♭7
See the girl with cym-bals on her fin-gers
Now she's danc-ing go-ing through the move-ments
Now she's mov-ing all a-round the ta-bles
en-ter-ing through the door
sway-ing to and fro
lur-ing all in sight
Ru-bies glis-ten-ing
Bo-dy mov-ing
But I know that
from_ her_ na-vel shim-mer-ing a-round the floor
bring-ing back a mem-o-ry thoughts of long a-go
she_ can-not see me hid-den by the light

Bells on feet go ting - a ling - a ling - ing go - ing through my
Blood is rush - ing tem - pra-ture's ris - ing sweat - ing from my
Clos - er clos - er she is get - ting near - er soon she'll be in
head
brow
reach
Sweat is fall - ing just - a like - a tear - drops
Like a snake her bo - dy fas - cin - ates me
As I en - ter in - to her spot - light
run - ning from her head
I can't look a - way
she stands lost for
1
2,3
now
speech

A♭
B♭
Stop stop stop all the danc - ing give me time to
breathe
A♭
Stop stop stop all the danc - ing
B♭
E♭7
To Coda
or I'll have to leave.
D.S. al Coda

CODA
E♭7
Now I held her peo - ple are star - ing
don't know what to think
And we strug - gle
knock-ing ov - er ta - bles spill - ing all the drinks

Can't they un - der - stand_ that I want her hap - pens ev - 'ry
week. Heav - y hand up - on __ my __ col - lar
Ab
throws me in the street Stop stop
Bb
stop all the danc - ing give me time to breathe

A♭
B♭
Stop stop stop all the danc - ing or I'll have to
E♭7
leave
Repeat and Fade

THE STROLL

With a moderately strong rock beat

Words and Music by
CLYDE OTIS and NANCY LEE

Bb7
F6
F6
let's stroll once more.
I feel so good
take me by the hand
I
Bb7
F6
feel so good
take me by the hand
C7
Bb7
And let's go stroll - ing in won - der

F6
land
Stroll - ing
Bb7
stroll - ing
Rock and
F6
roll - ing.
Bb7
Stroll - ing
C7
Well - a rock - a - my soul
Bb7
How I love to

F6
stroll
There's my love
stroll-ing in the door
Bb7
There's my love
stroll-ing in the door
F6
C7
Bb7
Ba-by, let's go stroll - ing by the can - dy
1 F6
store.
2 F6
store.

SUMMERTIME BLUES

Words and Music by
EDDIE COCHRAN and JERRY CAPEHART

F
time I call my Ba - by, Try to get a date, My Boss says, "No dice, Son, you
F
G7
got - ta work late." Some-times I won - der what I'm a - gon - na do But there
C
G7
C
F
ain't no cure for the sum - mer - time blues.
G
C
F
G
C
A well my

C
Mom 'n' Pa - pa told me, "Son, you got - ta make some mon - ey,
take two weeks Gon - na have a fine va - ca - tion,
F G C
If you want - ta use the car to go a -
I'm gon - na take my prob - lem to the
F G C
rid - in' next Sun - day,"
U - nit - ed Na - tions!
Well, I
Well, I
F
did - n't go to work Told the Boss I was sick "Now you
call my Con - gress - man and He said quote "I'd

can't___ use the car 'cause you did - n't work a lick"
like to help you, Son, but you're too young to vote"
F
G7
C
Some-times I won-der what I'm a - gon - na do___ But there ain't no cure for the
G7
C
2
F
G
C
sum-mer - times___ blues.
I'm gon - na
3
F
G
C
F
G
C

SWEET NOTHIN'S

Words and Music by
RONNIE SELF

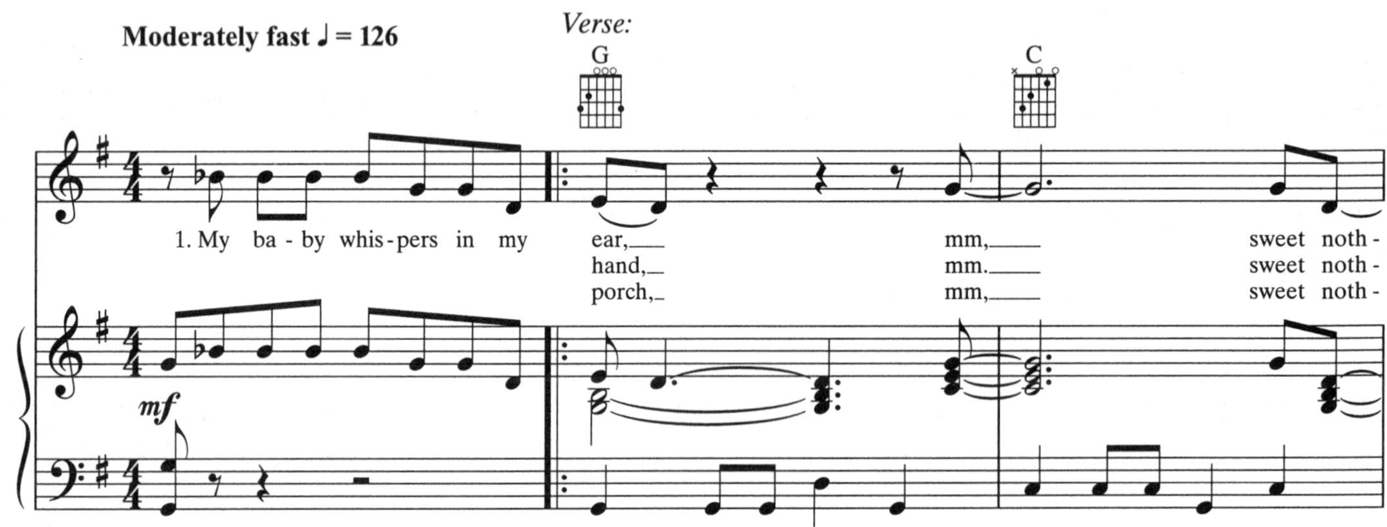
Moderately fast ♩ = 126
Verse:
G
C
1. My ba - by whis - pers in my ear,___ mm,___ sweet noth -
hand,___ mm.___ sweet noth -
porch,___ mm,___ sweet noth -
mf

G
in's. He knows the things I like to hear, mm,___
in's. Yeah, we both___ un - der - stand, mm,___
in's. Well, do I love you of___ course, mm,___

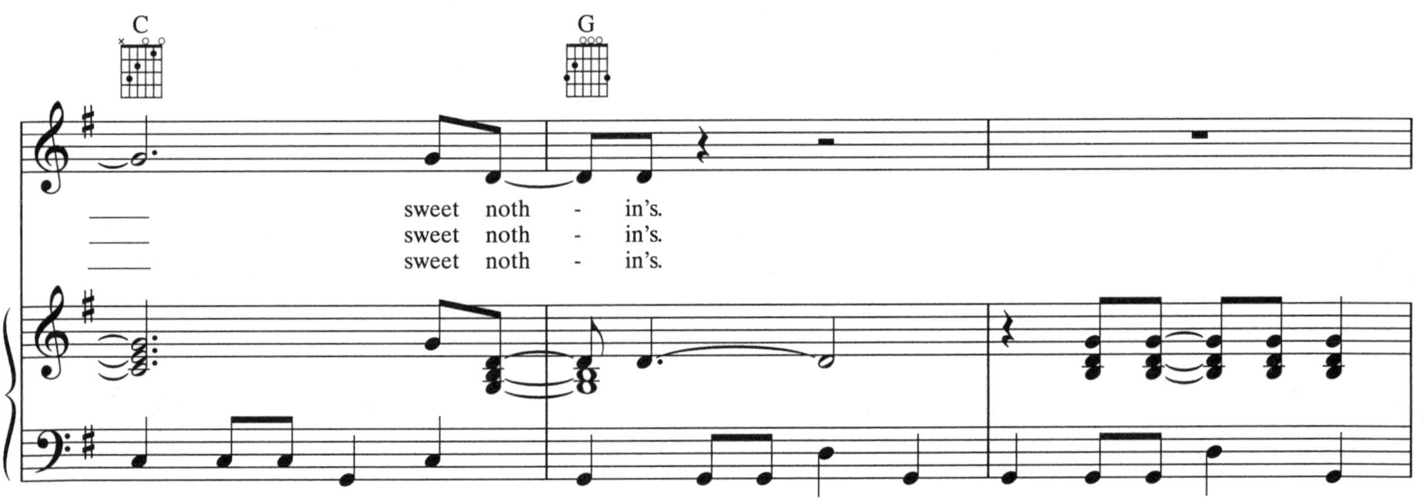
C
G
sweet noth - in's.
sweet noth - in's.
sweet noth - in's.

C
G
N.C.
Things he would - n't tell no - bod - y else.
Se - cret ba - by, I
Sit - tin' in class - room, try'n' to read my book,
my ba - by give me
Ma - ma turned_ on the front porch light, saying,
"Come in, dar - lin', that's
D7
C
G
keep them to my - self. Sweet noth - in's, mm,___ sweet noth - in's.
that spe - cial look.
...end solo)
e - nough for the night."
1.3.
N.C.
2.
4.
2. We walk a - long hand in
4. Sit - ting on my front
3. Inst. solo ad lib....
Sweet noth -
in's, mm,___ sweet noth - in's.
Sweet nothin's.

A TEENAGER IN LOVE

Words and Music by
DOC POMUS and MORT SHUMAN

Moderately Slow
mp
CHORUS
C
Am
F
G7
Each time we have a quar - rel it al - most breaks my heart,
One day I feel so hap - py; next day I feel so sad.
C
Am
F
G7
'Cause I am so a - fraid that we will have to part.
I guess I'll learn to take the good with the bad.
C
Am
F
G7
Each night I ask the stars up a - bove:

C (tacet)
G7
Why must I be a teen - ag - er in love?
246
F
G7
F
G7
I cried a tear for no - bod - y but you.
F
G7
F
G7
I'll be a lone - ly one if you should say we're through.
C
Am
F
G7
If you want to make me cry, that won't be so hard to do.

C
Am
F
G7
And if you should say good-bye, I'll still go on lov - ing you.
C
Am
F
G7
Each night I ask the stars up a - bove:
C
(tacet)
G7
Why must I be a teen - ag - er in love, in
1
C
F7
G7
love?
2
C
F7
C
love?

THIS DIAMOND RING

Words and Music by
BOB BRASS, AL KOOPER
and IRWIN LEVINE

Moderately
no chord
p

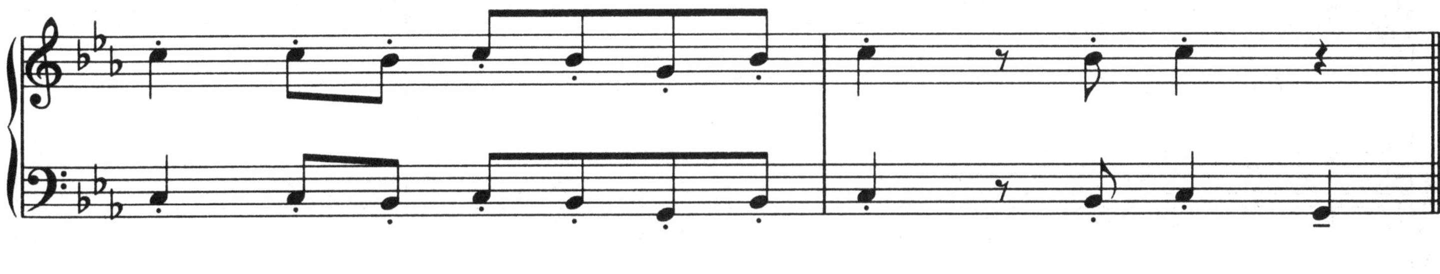

C
Eb
F
Who wants to buy this dia - mond ring?
This stone is gen - u - ine like love should be.

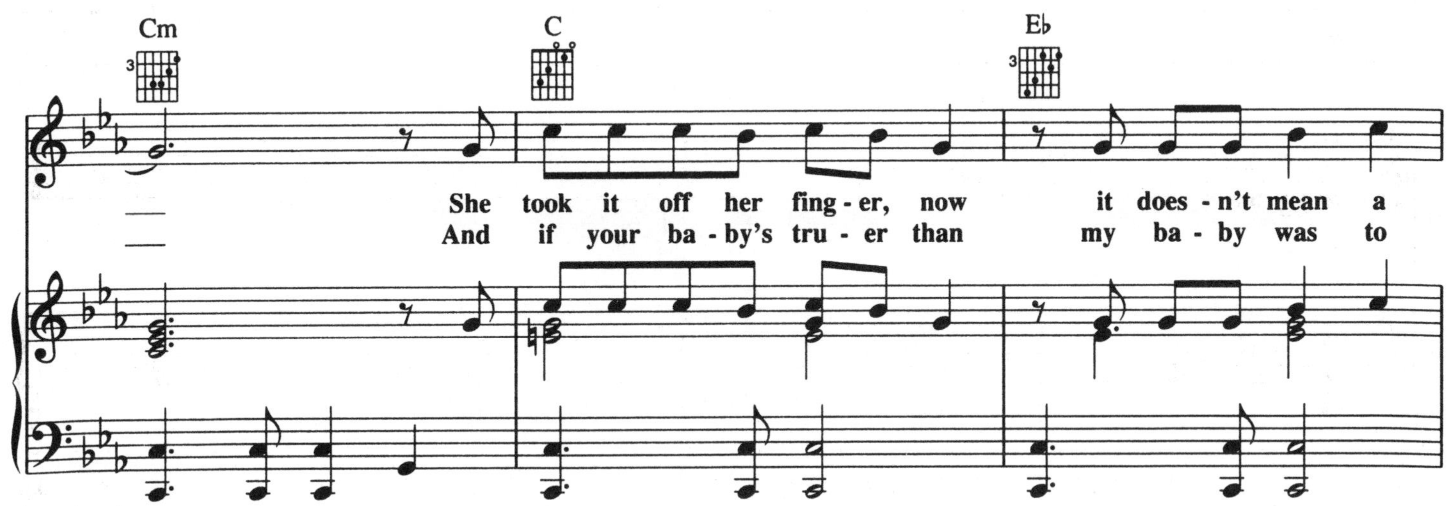
Cm
C
Eb
She took it off her fing - er, now it does - n't mean a
And if your ba - by's tru - er than my ba - by was to

F
D♭7
G♭
B♭m
thing.
me.
This dia-mond ring does-n't
This dia-mond ring can
E♭m
G♭
E♭m
G♭
B♭m
shine for me an-y-more, And this dia-mond ring does-n't
be some-thing beau-ti-ful, And this dia-mond ring can be
E♭m
G♭
G♭+
E♭m
B♭m
mean what it meant be-fore, So if you've got some-
dreams that are com-ing true, And then your heart won't
E♭m
B♭m
A♭m7
one whose love is true,
have to break like mine did,

D♭7
G♭
Let it shine for you.
If there's love be - hind it.
G
G7
Dm7
G7
C
E♭
Who wants to buy this dia - mond
F
Cm
Repeat and Fade
ring?

TILL THEN

Words and Music by
GUY WOOD, EDDIE SEILER and SOL MARCUS

Gm6
A7+5
Edim
B♭6
Bdim
F6
D7♭9
Gm
B♭m
when it will be, one day we'll be to-geth-er a-gain, please wait TILL
C9
Edim
Fmaj.7
F6
Gm7
C9
C7+5
Fmaj.7
F6
THEN. Our dreams will live tho' we are a-part, our love I know will
Gm6
A7+5
Edim
B♭6
Bdim
F6
D7♭9
keep in our hearts, TILL THEN please think of me lov-ing-ly, and
Gm
C9
F
E7
Am
E7
wait for me. Al-though there are o-ceans we must cross, and

Am
Bm7
E7
Am
E7
moun-tains that we must climb, I know ev-'ry gain must have a loss, so
Am7
Gm7
C9
Edim
Fmaj.7
F6
Gm7
C9
C7+5
pray that our loss is noth-ing but time. TILL THEN let's dream of what there will be, TILL
Fmaj.7
F6
Gm6
A7+5
Edim
B♭6
Bdim
Fmaj.7
Cm6
Adim
THEN we'll call on each mem-o-ry, TILL THEN when I will hold you a-gain, please
mf
1. Gm7
C9
F
D♭7
C7
2. Gm7
C7
F
wait TILL THEN. TILL wait TILL THEN.
rall.
f

TIME IS ON MY SIDE

Words and Music by
JERRY RAGOVOY

Slowly

Eb Ab Fm7 Bb9

mf

Eb Ab Fm7 Bb9

Eb Ab Bb7

Time ___ is on my side. ___ *(Spoken:) Yes, it is!*

Eb Ab Bb7

Time ___ is on my side. ___ *(Spoken:) Yes, it is!*

Cm
Gm
Cm
F7
Now, you were say - ing that you want to be free, but
You're search - ing for good times but just wait and see,
'Cause I got the real love the kind that you need,
Bb
Ab
Bb
Ab
You'll come run-ning back, you'll come run-ning back,
Bb
Ab
Bb
Ab
Bb7
To Coda
you'll come run-ning back, to me.
Ab
Eb
(Spoken:) Go ahead, go ahead and light up the town.

A♭
E♭
Baby, do everything your heart desires. Remember, I'll always be around.
A♭
Cm
And I know, like I told you so many times before. You're gonna come back, baby,
F7
B♭
D.S. al Coda
you're gonna come back knockin' right on my door!
CODA
E♭
A♭
B♭7
Repeat and Fade
Time, time, time, is on my side. (Spoken:) Yes it is!

TOSSIN' AND TURNIN'

Words and Music by
MALOU RENE and RITCHIE ADAMS

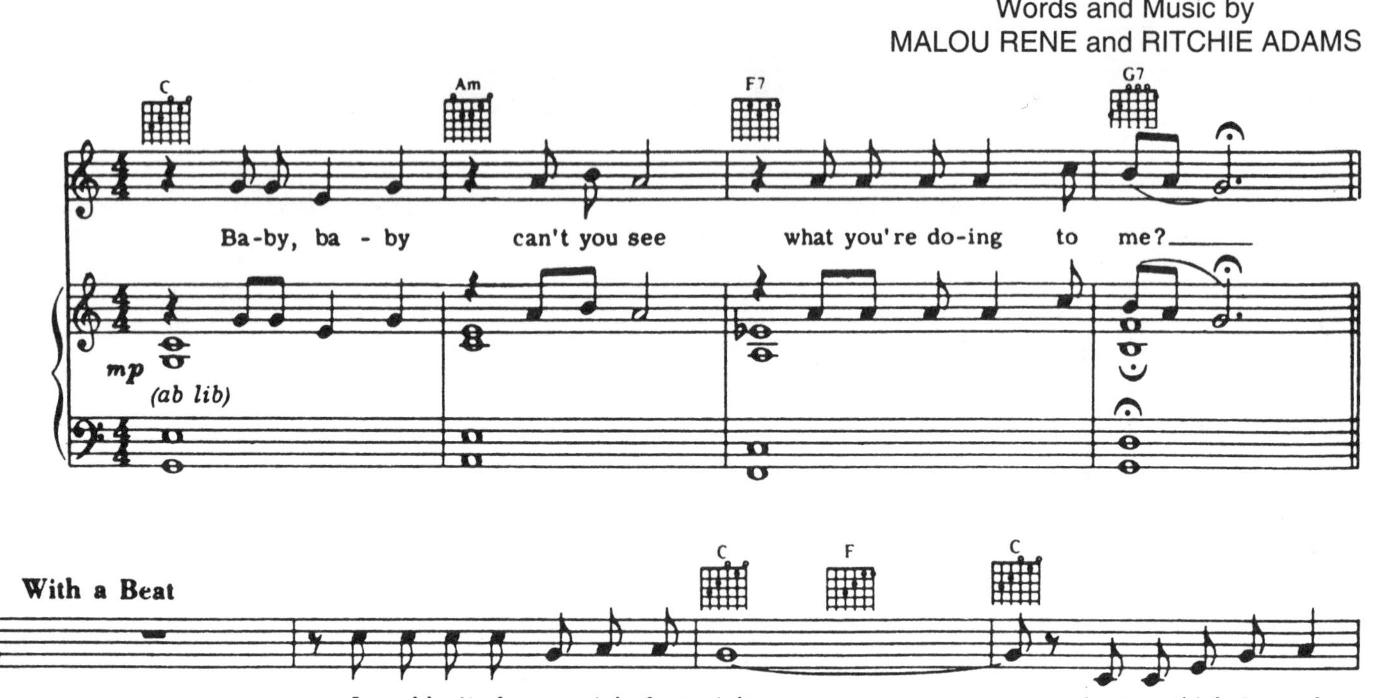

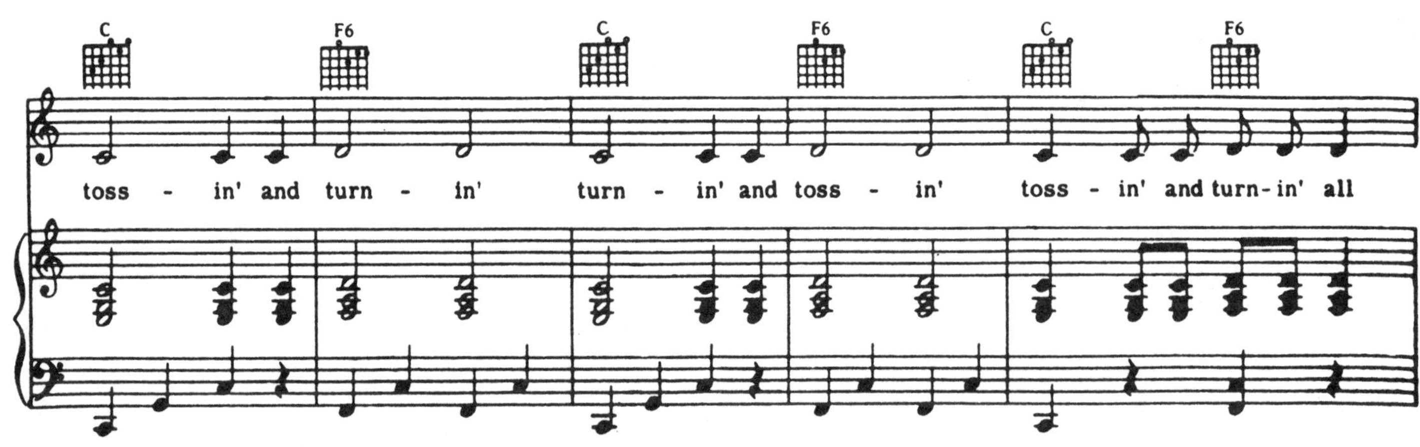

C
C
F
C
F
night. I threw the blank-ets on the floor,
turned my pil - low up - side down,
C
G7
C
Then I thought of you some more
And I kept on toss - in' and
F6
C
F6
C
F6
C
turn - in' turn - in' and toss - in' toss - in' and turn-in' all night.
F
C
Jumped out of bed, turned on the light, Pulled down the shade went to the

F
kitch-en for a bite. Pulled up the shade, turned off the light, I
D7
G7
jumped back in - to bed it was the mid-dle of the night.
C
F
C
C
F
The clock down-stairs was strik - ing four,
could-n't get you off my mind.
C
G7
C
Heard the milk-man at the door
but I was toss - in' and
F6
C
F6
C
F6
C
turn - in' turn - in' and toss - in' toss - in' and turn-in' all night.

TREAT HER LIKE A LADY

Words and Music by
EDDIE CORNELIUS

G
Am
Em
Treat Her Like A La - dy, - she'll give in to you. Lord, — you can seek, -
Treat Her Like A La - dy, - she'll give in to you. Lord, — you can seek, -
Treat Her Like A La - dy, — she'll give in to me. Lord, — you can seek, -
To Coda
1.
2.
Tacet
you know what I mean. I know you've
you know what I mean. Oh, - you've got to love her, tease —
you know what I
f
— her, but most of all you've got to please — her. You've got to
hold her and want — her and make her feel you'll al - ways need — her. You know a
wom-an is sen - ti - men-tal and so eas - y to up - set. — So make her

G
Am
Em
feel that she's for real and she'll give you hap-pi - ness. Wo, oh, oh,
E
D.S. al Coda
strange as it seems, you know you can't treat a wom-an mean. So my
mp
mf
D.S. al Coda
Coda
Tacet
G
Am
mean. Oh, you've got - ta Treat Her Like A La - dy,
Repeat and fade
G
Am
G
do the best you can do. You got - ta Treat Her Like A La -
Am
Em
- dy, she'll give in to you. You got to

WATERLOO

Words and Music by
JOHN LOUDERMILK and MARIJOHN WILKIN

Eb
Ab
Eb
Bb
To Coda
1
Eb
pup-py has it's day ev-'ry bo-dy has to pay. Ev-'ry bo-dy has to meet his Wa-ter - loo. Lit-tle
2
Eb
Ab
Eb
loo. Now a fel-lah who's dar-lin' proved un-true. Took her life but
F
Bb
Eb
Ab
Eb
he lost his too. Now he swings where the lit- tle bird - ies sing, and that's
Bb
Eb
D.S. al Coda
CODA
Eb
where Tom Doo-ley met his Wa - ter - loo. Wa - ter - loo.

TURN ME LOOSE

Words and Music by
DOC POMUS and MORT SHUMAN

Moderately slow
mf
G
G7
C7
Turn me loose, turn me loose, I say, This is the first time I ev - er
C#dim
G
D7
D7sus
felt this way. Gon - na get a thou - sand kicks, gon - na kiss a thou - sand chicks, So turn me
G
D7
G
loose. Turn me loose, turn me

G7
C7
C#dim
loose, I say.
Gon-na rock and roll long as the band's gon-na play. Gon-na
G
D7
D7sus
G
C
hol-ler, gon-na shout, knock my-self right out, So turn me loose.
G
Guitar Tacet
C
I got some change in my pock-et and I'm rar-in' to go. I'm
G
A7
tak-in' some chick to the pic-ture show, When I see her home and we

D7
kiss good-night, Turn me loose, turn me loose, turn me loose, turn me loose. Turn me
G
G7
C7
loose, turn me loose, I say.
Yes, to-day is gon-na
C#dim
G
D7
D7sus
be the day. I want you all to un-der-stand that now I am a man, so turn me
1
G
C7
D7
2
G
C7
G
loose. Turn me loose.

WHAT THE WORLD NEEDS NOW IS LOVE

Words by
HAL DAVID

Music by
BURT BACHARACH

Em7
C6
3rd time to Coda
B
love, No, not just for some, but for ev - 'ry - one.
B7
Em7
Lord, we don't need an - oth - er moun - tain,
Lord, we don't need an - oth - er mead - ow,
Dm9
G9/6
There are moun - tains and hill - sides e -
There are corn - fields and wheat - fields e -
Cmaj7
C6
Dm7
nough to climb; There are o - ceans and
nough to grow; There are sun - beams and

G9/6
Cmaj7
Em7
riv - ers e - nough to cross, E - nough to last
moon - beams e - nough to shine, Oh, lis - ten, Lord,
A7
D9
Am7/D
till the end of time.
if you want to know. What the
Coda
B
B7
E7
C6
C
ev - 'ry-one. No, not just for some, Oh, but
Bm7
Cmaj7
D7
G
just for ev - 'ry - one.

WHAT'D I SAY

Words and Music by
RAY CHARLES

C7
Bb7
F7
F
right, now.
right, now.
right.
Tell me WHAT'D I
F
SAY?
Tell me WHAT'D I
SAY right now?
Tell me WHAT'D I
know,
I wan - na
know.
Ba - by, I wan-na
Bb7
F
SAY?
Tell me WHAT'D I
SAY?
Tell me WHAT'D I
know right now,
Yes, I wan - na
know.
Hon-ey, I wan-na
C7
Bb7
F
1
SAY?
Tell me WHAT'D I
SAY?
Yes, I wan - na
know,
Yes, I wan - na
know.

2
F
Hey, (Hey) ho, (ho) hey, (hey)
Hey, (Hey) ho, (ho) hey, (hey)
Huh, (Huh) ho, (ho) huh, (huh)
f
ho, (ho) hey, (hey) ho, (ho) hey, Sing me one more
ho, (ho) hey, (hey) ho, (ho) hey, Make me feel so
ho, (ho) huh, (huh) ho, (ho) huh, Ba - by, it's all
F
time, Sing me one more time, Sing me one more
good, Make me feel so good, Make me feel so
right, Ba - by, it's all right, right now, Ba - by it's all
mf
Bb7
F
time, Sing me one more time, Sing me one more
good right now, Make me feel so good, Make me feel so
right, Ba - by, it's all right, Ba - by, it's all

C7
Bb7
F
1-2
3
time, Sing me one more time.
good, Make me feel so good.
right, Ba - by, it's all right. Come on, twist that
f
F
thing, Come on, twist that thing, Keep a - twist- in' that
right, Well, I feel all right, Well, I feel all
Bb7
F
thing, Keep a - twist - in' that thing, Keep a - twist-in' that
right, Well, I feel all right, Well, I feel all
C7
Bb7
F
1
2
thing, Keep a - twist- in' that thing. Make me feel all
right, Well, I feel all right.

WHY

Words and Music by
BOB MARCUCCI and
PETER DeANGELIS

Cm7
oth - er.
And with our faith and
Bb
Am7
D7
trust, there could be no oth - er,
why, 'cause I love you,
Am7
D7
G
Gmaj7
G6
Gmaj7
why, 'cause you love me. I think you're aw - f'ly sweet, why, be- cause I
Am7
D7
Am7
D7
Am7
D7
love you.
You say I'm your spe- cial

Am7
D7
G
Gmaj7
G6
Gmaj7
Dm7
treat, why, be-cause you love me.
We found a per-fect
C
Cm6
love, yes, a love that's yours and mine.
G
Gmaj7
Am7
D7
1 G
Gdim7
I love you and you love me all the time.
Am7
D9
D7♭9
2 G
time.

YOU BABY
(Nobody But You)

Words and Music by
P.F. SLOAN and STEVE BARRI

C♯m
E
F♯
feel like smil - in' when the wea-ry day is through.
Chorus:
B E F♯ E B E
ff
You ba - by no one but you ba - by no -
F♯ E B E F♯ E
bod - y but you. You ba - by no one but
B E
you ba - by no -
1. F♯ E B N.C.
D.C.
bod - y but you.
2. F♯ E B N.C.
bod - y but you.
Interlude:
B
mf
A lit - tle ray of sun-

Verse 2:
They say candy is sweet,
But it just can't compete with you baby.
You've got everything I need,
And nobody can please like you do baby.
(Nobody but you.)

Bridge 2:
And who believes, that my wildest dreams,
And my craziest schemes will come true.
(To Chorus:)

YOU DON'T OWN ME

Words and Music by
JOHN MADARA and DAVE WHITE

2
B♭
boys.
stay.
And
I
don't
don't
tell
tell
me
you
what
what
to
to
do,
say,
Gm
I
Don't
don't
tell
tell
me
you
what
what
to
to
say;
do;
E♭
And
So
please
just
when
I
go
let
me

F7
out with you,
be my - self,
Don't
That's
put
all
me
I
To Coda
Bbm
D.S. al Coda
on dis - play.
ask of you.
'Cause,
You
don't
CODA
Bb
I'm
young
and
I
Gm
love to be young,
I'm
free
and
I

E♭
love to be free; To live my
life the way that I want, To
F7
say and do what - ev - er I please.
B♭m
E♭m
F7
Repeat and Fade
You don't own me.

YOU REALLY GOT ME

Words and Music by
RAY DAVIES

G F G F G F G F G
got me now You got me so I don't know what I'm do-ing - Oh
C Bb C Bb C Bb C Bb C Bb C Bb
yeah you real-ly got me now - You got me so I can't sleep at night you
C Bb C Bb C Bb C Bb C Bb C Bb Bb
real-ly got me - You real-ly got me - You real-ly got me -
C Bb C
Oh oh -

YOU'LL NEVER NEVER KNOW

Words and Music by
PAUL ROBI, JEAN MILES and TONY WILLIAMS

E7
A
D
Oh, no, you'll nev - er ___ nev - er know.
You'll nev-er nev-er see me
F#7
Bm
F#7
cry, ___
not ___ e - ven when you're glanc-ing by.
G
Gm
D
E7
A
For ___ I won't weak-en when we're speak-ing.
Oh, oh, you'll nev - er ___ nev - er
D
D7
know. ___ You'll know the used to be that

G
E7
I was be - fore.
You'll see the
Em7
A
used to be that one you did a - dore.
D
F#7
Bm
No, no, oh, no I won't re - veal
oh no you'll nev - er tru - ly
F#7
G
Gm
D
feel.
But if you guess it
I'll con- fess it.

E7
F#
Oh, dar - ling, now's the time to glow
1 G
G/A
D
or else you'll nev - er nev - er know. You
2 G
G/A
G
G/A
G
G/A
or else you'll nev - er, no no you'll nev - er, oh no you'll
no chord
D
ev - er know. Oo.

YOU'RE MY WORLD

Original Words and Music by
UMBERTO BINDI and GINO PAOLI
English Lyric by CARL SIGMAN

Moderately slow ♩. = 69

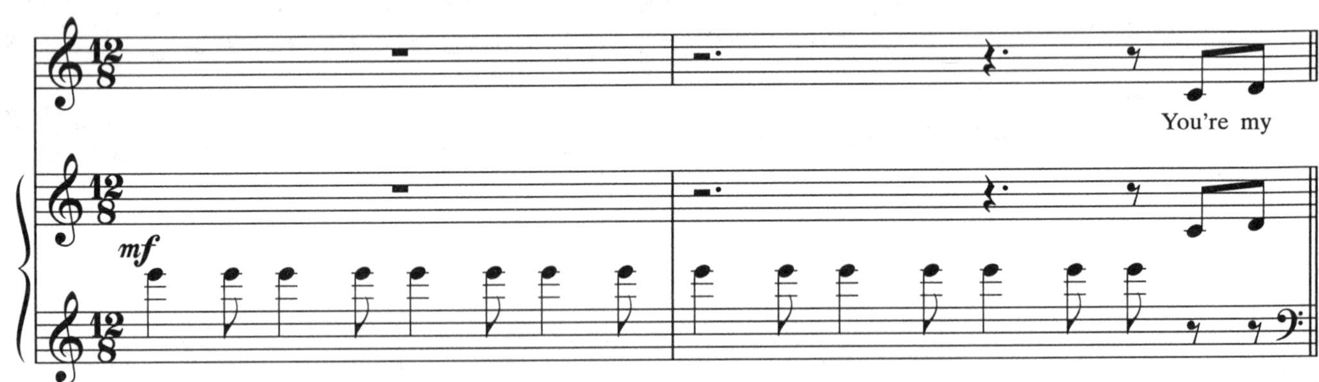
mf
You're my

Verse:

*Am
D
G7
world, you're_ ev-'ry breath I take.
You're my world, you're_ ev-'ry move I

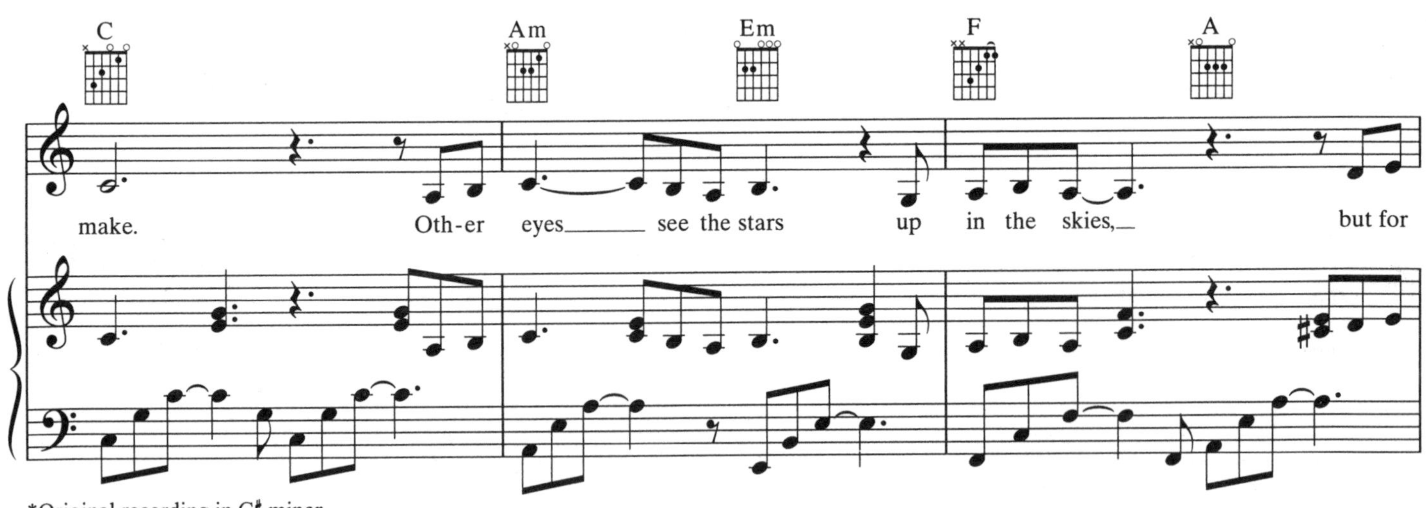
C
Am
Em
F
A
make. Oth-er eyes_____ see the stars up in the skies,_ but for

*Original recording in G♯ minor.

Dm
G7
C
E7sus
E7
Am
me, they shine with - in your eyes. As the trees reach for the sun a -
D
G7
C
bove, so my arms reach out to you for love. With your
Bridge:
F
C
G7
hand rest - ing in mine, I feel a
C
E7
A
E7sus
E7
pow - er so di - vine. You're my

Chorus:

A F♯m7 D Bm7

world, you are my night ___ and day. ___ You're my

Bm7/E E7 A

world, you're ev - 'ry prayer ___ I pray. ___ If our

D Dm6 A/E Dm6/F

love ___ ceas - es to be, then it's the

1.

Bm7/E E7 **Freely** Am

end of ___ my world, ___ for me.

D
G7
C
With your
2.
A/E
Bm7/E
A/E
Bm7/E
end of my world,
end of my world,
A/E
N.C.
Bm7/E
E7
A
F♯m7
end of my world for me.
D
Bm7
Bm7/E
A
rit.

YOU'RE THE ONE

Words and Music by
TONY HATCH, PETULA CLARK
and GEORGES ABER

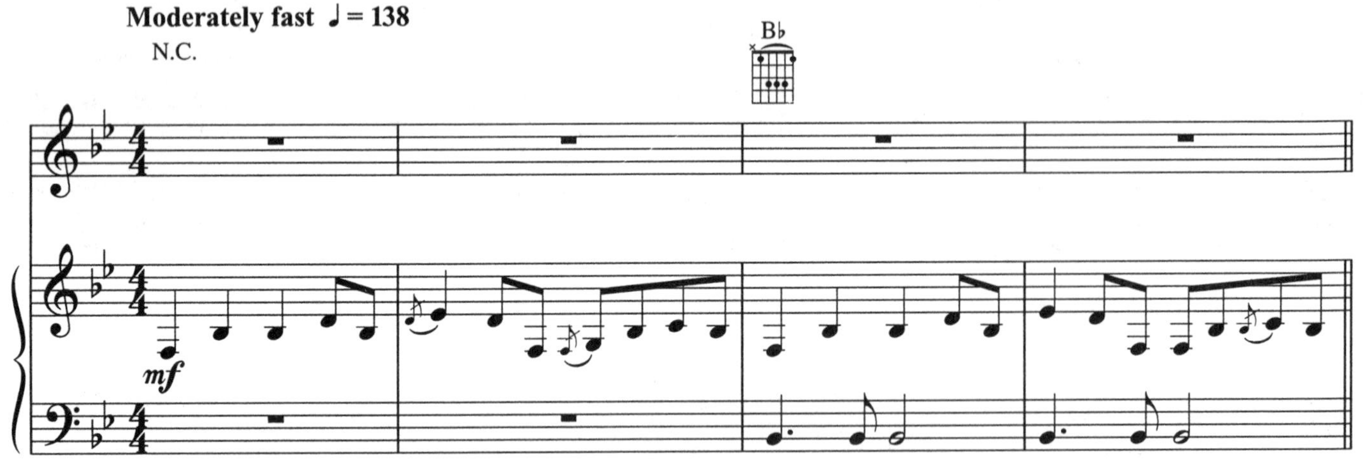
Moderately fast ♩ = 138
N.C.
B♭
mf

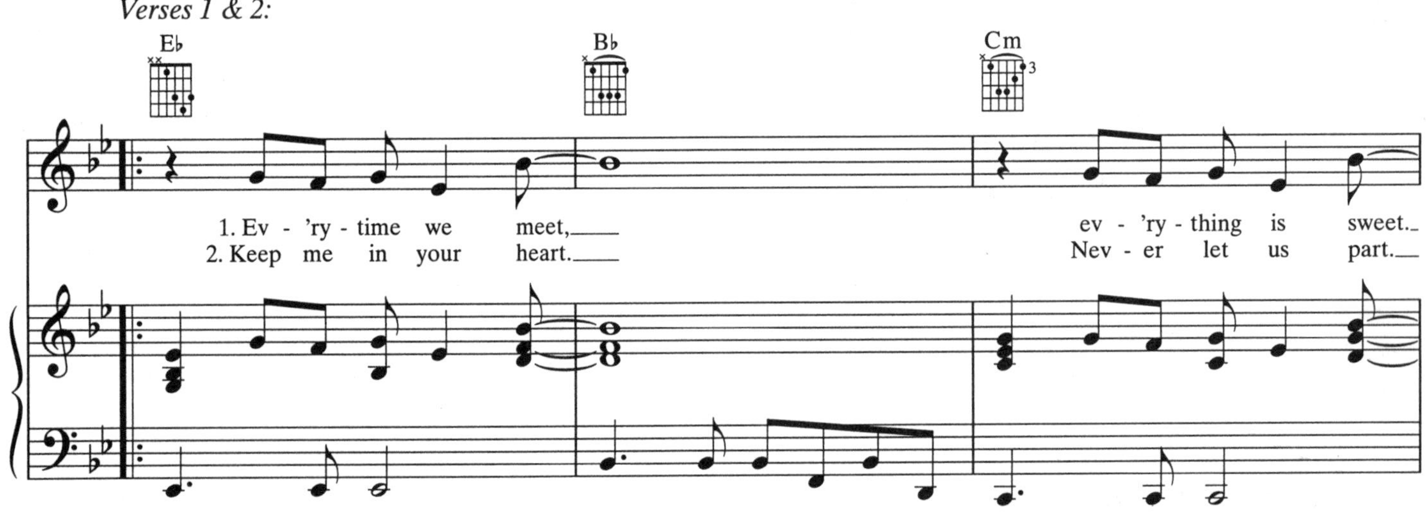
Verses 1 & 2:
E♭
B♭
Cm
1. Ev - 'ry - time we meet,
ev - 'ry - thing is sweet.
2. Keep me in your heart.
Nev - er let us part.

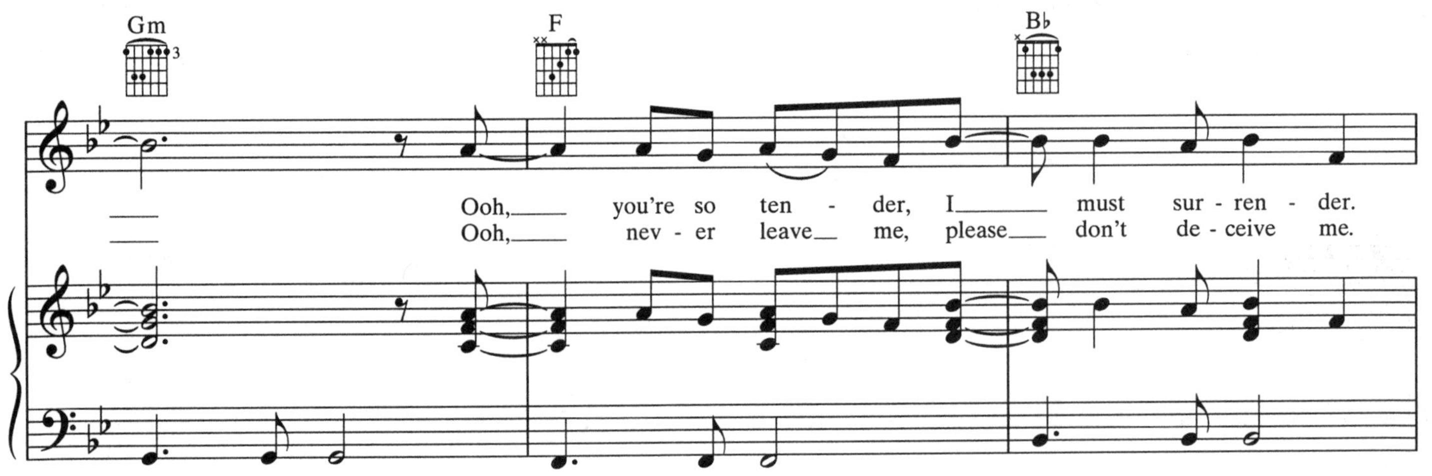
Gm
F
B♭
Ooh, you're so ten - der, I must sur - ren - der.
Ooh, nev - er leave me, please don't de - ceive me.

𝄋 *Chorus:*

E♭ F B♭

My love is your love, now___ and for - ev - er. (1.2.) You're the one___ that I
I want you on - ly, you___ must be - lieve___ me. (3.) *(Inst. solo ad lib....*

E♭ F B♭

long to kiss.___ Ba - by, you're the one___ that I real - ly miss.___

E♭ F *To Coda* 𝄌

You're the one___ that I'm dream - ing of.___ Ba - by, you're the one___ that I

1. B♭ 2. B♭

love.___ love.___

Bridge:
F
E♭/F
F
E♭/F
F
E♭/F
I a - dore you, and no one be - fore you could make me feel this
Gm
E♭
way.
Since I met you, I just can't for - get you. I
F
D.S. 𝄋 al Coda
love you more each day,
yeah, yeah, yeah, yeah.
Coda
B♭ N.C.
Verse 3:
E
B
...end solo)
3. There may be some tears

C♯m
G♯m
F♯
though the com - ing years.
Ooh, all the while I know
B
E
F♯
you'll be smil - ing. Your love will guide me through ev - 'ry mile, 'cause…
Chorus:
B
E
F♯
B
You're the one that I long to kiss. Ba - by, you're the one that I real - ly miss.
Repeat ad lib. and fade
E
F♯
B
You're the one that I'm dream - ing of. Ba - by, you're the one that I love.

GO WHERE YOU WANNA GO

Words and Music by
JOHN PHILLIPS

G
C
G
C
G
do what you wan-na do with whom - ev- er you wan - na do it, babe.
G
D
Em
C
You don't un - der - stand that a girl like me can love
D
just one man.
G
F
Em
Three thou - sand miles, that's how far you'll
You've been gone a week and I've tried so

D
Em
To Coda
A7
D7
G
go,
hard
And you said to me
Not to be the cry
Please
Em
D
don't go.
You've got - ta
G
C
go where you wan-na go,
do what you wan-na do
with whom-ev - er you wan - na do
no chord
it, babe.
You've got-ta go where you wan-na go,
do what you wan-na do with

G
C
G
D.S. al Coda
CODA
A7
D7
whom-ev - er you wan-na do it!
- in' kind,
G
Em
A
Not to be the girl you left be - hind.
D
G
C
Go where you wan-na go,
G
C
G
C
G
Repeat and Fade
do what you wan - na do with whom-ev - er you wan - na do it.

YOU'RE SIXTEEN

Words and Music by
RICHARD M. SHERMAN and
ROBERT B. SHERMAN

C
Am7
D7
G9
G7
C
F
shine. You're six - teen you're beau - ti - ful and you're mine.
C
G7
C
You're my ba - by, you're my pet. We fell in love on the
D9
night we met. You touched my hand, my heart went 'pop', And
G6(add9)
G9
G6(add9)
C
ooh, when we kissed we could not stop, You walked out of my dreams,

E7
F
C
Am7
in - to my arms,
now you're my an - gel di - vine.
You're six - teen,
D7
1
G9
G7
C
Am
Dm7
G6(add9)
you're beau - ti - ful and you're mine.
Ooh, you come
2
G9
G7
G9
C
B7
B♭7
A7
beau - ti - ful and you're mine.
Ooh
you're
Dm7
G9
C
beau - ti - ful, You're six - teen and you're mine.